Saving Buddy

NICOLA OWST

Saving Buddy

NICOLA OWST

MIRROR BOOKS

Contents

First published by Mirror Books in 2019

Mirror Books is part of Reach plc
10 Lower Thames Street
London EC3R 6EN
England

www.mirrorbooks.co.uk

ISBN 978-1-912624-66-9

1 3 5 7 9 10 8 6 4 2

To all my friends and
family who have had a
positive impact on my life.
You know who you are.

Finding Buddy

The sat nav told us we'd reached our destination. Surely, I thought, this couldn't be the right place. The rain was pelting down. It was the kind of storm where it feels as if buckets of water are literally being chucked at the windscreen. No matter how hard we tried, it was impossible to make out any road signs and work out where we were.

It was the morning of Monday 27 April 2009. We'd been heading south towards London and had turned off the M1 around an hour earlier. Since then, the journey had felt relentless. We'd turned second left here, third right there, down tiny B roads and up muddy farm tracks. It seemed as if we were just moving further and further into the middle of nowhere. It felt quite exciting to be involved in such a complex mystery tour, and yet more than a little bit unnerving at the same time.

We were there to pick up a foal that was no longer wanted by its owner. Sally had contacted him via the internet as she ran a stables just outside Leicester and didn't bat an eyelid about traipsing up and down the country in all weathers if it meant that she could improve the life of a horse.

Owners would contact her via her website. She would either rehouse the horses or she would liaise with people who considered buying the horses once they'd regained their health and fitness at her stables.

I'd been on several similar trips with Sally and her teenage daughter Charlie in the past – and it was always an adventure. We'd set off early in the morning, armed with flasks of tea, cheese sandwiches, a bag of cherry tomatoes and a tub of hummus, and maybe the odd cheeky packet or two of Haribo in the glove compartment.

We'd all pile into Sally's four-by-four – me and Sally in the front, Charlie in the back, and Sally's beautiful dogs, her Rhodesian Ridgeback, Scamp, and her Doberman, Zeus, in the boot. Off we'd go, the three of us nattering away about anything and everything, and laughing about the sat nav's accent. Why Sally never changed it I don't know. Hearing her questioning its directions was like listening to an old married couple bickering.

On this occasion though, I wondered if it could be curtains for Sally's relationship with the sat nav. It had directed us to some kind of no-man's-land, full of abandoned farm equipment, rusty bits of machinery, junk and piles of fly-tipped rubbish. There was graffiti everywhere, a circle of old chairs, discarded beer cans, cigarette butts and pieces of scaffolding.

It felt like we'd stumbled upon the meeting place for some kind of sinister society; it really was the grimmest, scariest place I'd ever been to. As the rain continued to lash down, suddenly this adventure didn't seem like fun any more. What had we managed to get ourselves into?

Sally phoned the foal's owner. He gruffly told her that he would be with us in a few minutes, but we were beginning to have second thoughts. It just didn't feel right. Even Scamp and Zeus could tell this was a bad place. With their ears pricked up and their nostrils flaring, they could sense the aggression in the air. It was all very unsettling.

The foal we were meant to be picking up was a six-month-old bay colt. Its owner wanted to get rid of him, so it was Sally to the rescue yet again. As the three of us waited for the horse's owner to arrive, we anxiously kept looking at each other. I'm sure we were all thinking the same thing: how quickly can we get out of this godforsaken place?

Just as we were about to turn around and abandon the mission, a shady-looking middle-aged man ambled towards us. There was a younger guy with him who looked as if he could be the man's son, but there was no sign of the foal. When Sally wound down the window to ask them where we should be heading, the middle-aged man pointed to a nearby area of scrubland.

This really isn't a good idea, I thought. It was obviously not a proper paddock. It had quite a severe dip in the middle of it, and a horse could have easily fallen down and injured itself. It's safe to say that animal welfare wasn't high on the list of priorities for these two men.

Peering through the rain into the distance, we finally spotted the frail foal. We all climbed out of the car and began to get the horsebox ready, hoping it would be a simple matter of reining him in and then getting on our way. But as we battled through the storm, it took us a good hour to get the young colt to come anywhere near us.

It quickly became apparent that the colt had no trust in humans. It may have been mistreated, although we couldn't know for sure. And it certainly wasn't the time or place to start getting into discussions like that. The only thing that mattered there and then was rescuing the poor creature. But this wasn't an easy task.

Each time we would edge towards him, the colt would rear up and dart away. Even the most gentle coaxing with soft voices and a very slow approach didn't work. He didn't want to know. But Sally was the most experienced horse-woman I knew, and she wasn't going to give up.

When we did eventually manage to catch the foal and attach a lead rope to him, we saw that he was in a terrible state, severely underweight and obviously full of worms. He really did look as if he was on his last legs. There was no question of us leaving him there, even if ultimately we knew there was a good chance we wouldn't be able to save him.

Sally wordlessly handed over the cash to the man. No bartering was required. Ordinarily, when she went out to buy a horse, Sally would try to get to know more about the animal's temperament and history, but this was a mercy mission, pure and simple. We managed to load the young foal on to the trailer and gave him some hay to nibble on to distract him, and got ready to leave.

Just as we were finishing up, Sally spotted another foal in the field. A filly with a white blaze was looking in our direction. On impulse, Sally asked if the man would consider selling this horse too. The man shrugged and put out his hand for more money. He must have thought this was his lucky day – easy cash.

Although the other foal had been a challenge to round up, this one was easy to catch, but as the men tried to load it into the trailer, it just lay down and played dead. I'd lived and worked at the stables since my teens, and I'd never seen a horse behave like this before. I knew she wasn't dead, but she certainly wasn't in any mood to move either. Was this her way of saying she didn't want to leave this place? Or was she so desperate about her situation that it was all too much and she was just going to leave her future to fate?

Undeterred that the foal was acting strangely, the seller sent his companion to find a rope. Together, they roughly wrapped the rope around the half-starved creature. Then they literally dragged the dead weight up the ramp into the vehicle. It was really distressing to watch as they heaved her up the ramp like a lump of meat. We were all in shock, but there was no way we were going to get into a fight with these men.

To our delight, the foal had the last laugh. As the older man removed his rope from around her, she kicked out her back leg, landing her hoof right between his legs. If the man's mobile phone hadn't been deep inside his trouser pocket, it would have been a very eye-watering injury. He was furious that the foal had broken his phone's screen though, and he ranted and raved, looking as if he was about to give her a good kicking.

We needed to get out of there fast. So while Sally finished loading up the horsebox, I beckoned Charlie to come with me as she was understandably very upset about the whole situation. I was too. We needed some distance from these terrible people so that I could calm Charlie down. We headed back in the direction we'd come from, towards all of the rubbish and broken machinery.

I knew Sally would be fine. Scamp and Zeus had obviously got the measure of the two men. Given the signal, they wouldn't have hesitated to have leapt to her defence. I'd seen the men looking at the dogs with wariness and with what could even be described as fear, realising that they were our eight-legged protection team.

Charlie and I walked along quickly, too numb to say anything at first. What was there to say? We knew Sally was doing the right thing, and the sooner we could start caring for the foals, the better. Having been in rescue situations before, we'd encountered some incredibly cruel people. We like to tell ourselves that Britain is a nation of animal lovers. But there are people out there who can barely care for themselves, let alone any animals who have the misfortune to end up with them. We knew it wouldn't be the last time we'd be on a mission like this.

Some good would come out of that day though. Charlie was looking forward to settling in the foals at the stables, and she'd already thought up names for them. The most important thing now was to get them home and help them to start their new life.

Charlie and I were heading back to the car when, out of the corner of her eye, she spotted an animal wedged into the back of a crate. She ran over to investigate.

"Hey!" she shouted to us. "There's a dog in here and I think it's dead."

Sally and I immediately shushed her. The men weren't quite out of earshot yet, and we really didn't want to make any trouble with them. Our reactions to the way they'd manhandled the foals had obviously rubbed them up the wrong way. We guessed that things had the potential to get ugly if we weren't careful.

I squatted down and peered inside the rusty metal crate to see the dog more closely. The poor creature was squashed inside a cat carrier inside the crate. He looked as if he may have crawled in there to shelter from the rain and, as Charlie had said, he looked as if he was dead. Looking more closely though, I noticed the faintest signs of breathing. The poor creature's breath was too shallow to move his bony rib cage, but there was definitely something there. He was clinging on to life. But who knew how long he was going to survive?

Without thinking twice or telling Charlie what I was

going to do, I ran to the car and grabbed one of Scamp and Zeus's towels from the boot. Then I ran back to the metal crate. After freeing the cat box first, I put both of my hands around the dog's listless body and carefully lifted him out of his prison. He really was just a bag of bones. It felt like he only weighed seven or eight pounds at the most, even though he looked like he was quite a big, old dog.

I could see that he was some kind of Staffy-type dog. Looking at the terrible scarring all over his face, it was plain to see that he'd endured the most dreadful mistreatment. Had he been involved in illegal dog fights? Looking around the yard, it all seemed to add up. I could imagine those men being involved in something like that. To them, animals were obviously just a way to make money.

His poor sad eyes were just slits in his bony, bruised face. It looked as if just trying to keep them open was causing him intense pain, so he wasn't really opening his eyes at all. The skin around his filthy swollen muzzle was pockmarked and livid pink where his fur had worn away. It looked as if his flesh had been grated or clawed at. His skin was so paper-thin in some areas of his face that I could almost see through it.

Blood under his right eye had soaked down his face and neck and onto his body. Mottled flesh hung in folds around his skeletal bird-like legs, which showed every tendon and sinew. He was barely alive and looked as if he was wasting away. In some places on his legs there was no fur at all, just thin pink skin. Every movement he made seemed agonising for him.

He'd obviously had no food or water for days. He'd just been left there to die. Trapped in the cat carrier, he'd been shut away in his own waste. The stench was unbelievable, an awful combination of rotting flesh and faeces. His little paw pads were burnt and red raw from standing in his own urine. It was unbelievably sad. What kind of monster could leave an animal in such an awful state?

I'd never seen such neglect before, even in the worst animal cruelty cases I'd seen on television. I think I was in shock, and I don't remember the three of us exchanging a single word as I wrapped the dog in the towel and carried him out of the crate. It was just pitiful. There was no way I was going to leave him there.

Like Sally and the second foal, I didn't think twice about rescuing the poor dog. I could see that he was covered in mange – a nasty infection caused by mites that burrow under the skin. I knew there was a chance that I could catch the infection too, but that didn't matter in the slightest to me. The important thing was to try to do the best I could for this pitiful creature. When I lifted his limp, fragile body on to my lap, his legs buckled beneath him. He had no strength left. I gently swaddled him in the towel.

"I've got you now, buddy," I whispered to him. "You'll be okay."

From that moment on, he would always be known as Buddy.

Quietly, the three of us climbed into the car and set the sat nav for home. There was no arguing this time with its route for the journey back. What we'd gone through had put trivial things into perspective. All we wanted to do was see the sign for the M1, northbound, and know that we were properly on our way home.

I was renting a room at the stables at the time. I began to wonder what Sally's husband Rob would have to say when he found out that we were returning with not one, but two foals – plus a very poorly dog. At the time though, my biggest concern was how we'd get through the journey. I was worried Buddy might not even survive the two-hour journey back, as he seemed so close to death. And then what would we do with a dead dog's body?

Curled up on my lap asleep, the dog was now warm and dry, at the very least. I kept looking down at him and saying, "Hang in there, Buddy", as we trundled back along the various roads that would lead us home.

At one point, Sally turned to me and said, "What have

we done?"

I just shrugged at her. This was the only thing we could do. Leaving the animals there wasn't an option. There was no way we would ever just leave an animal to die. As to what would happen next, who knew? There was no point worrying about that now. I tried to ignore the fact that maybe I hadn't done the most sensible thing. I felt bad that it was my fault we were in this situation, but I knew Sally and Charlie would have done the same thing and brought Buddy back with us too. Trouble was, it wasn't just us in the car.

The one thing we couldn't possibly ignore was the smell. It was absolutely horrendous. Back in the boot, Scamp and Zeus were getting restless because of the putrid stench. It was so bad that after about two miles, Zeus started drooling furiously and was then violently sick. So now we also had the stink of vomit to put up with, as well as the excrement and Buddy's rancid skin. Could things get any worse? Winding down the windows didn't help, and anyway it was still pouring down with rain. So without saying anything, I think we all just tried to zone out from the smell until we could reach a service station and hopefully sort out the situation.

As soon as the sign for a service station came into view, we pulled in, parked up and seconds later went into action. Charlie took Scamp and Zeus to stretch their legs and get some air, and Sally opened up all of the windows and cleaned up the vomit. As I placed Buddy carefully on the front seat, he looked up at me as if to say, "Don't go." I reassured him that I would be back soon and then I headed for the loo.

As I walked through the service station, everyone – and I mean EVERYONE – turned towards me to see where the awful smell was coming from. Before I'd even seen the dog, I'd been wet through and had stepped in cowpats while rounding up the foals so you can imagine what state I was in. I felt like some kind of sewer rat dripping through the building. I tried to keep my head down, but people made no attempt to hide how disgusting I smelled as they pulled their jackets over their noses or dry-heaved as I went by.

I couldn't really blame them, but to be quite honest, I didn't care. I just wanted to have the quickest loo trip ever and to get back to my new best friend as soon as I could. As I opened the car door on my return, Buddy's little eyes looked up at me. I climbed back in the car and settled him on my lap. I already felt so protective of him and said, "Are you alright, my little Buddy?"

Safe and sound

Once we were back on the road, I phoned Ian Carpenter, the vet we often used at the stables, and asked if I could get an emergency appointment for Buddy. I also asked if I could come in through the back door of his surgery in Market Harborough, because the dog and I were in such a bad condition. The situation was stressful enough without more people having to put up with the smell of us and expressing their disgust. There was also the chance that someone may have thought I was the cause of Buddy's pitiful state. It's quite a small town, and I wanted to avoid wasting time having to explain what had happened.

Thankfully, we had a relatively smooth 86-mile drive back to Market Harborough after the vomiting incident.

Sally dropped me at Ian's and then went back to the stables with Charlie to tell Rob about the day's adventures. Rob is very easygoing, and I knew he wouldn't mind that Sally had brought back two foals rather than just the one he was expecting. I wasn't quite so confident about Buddy though. When Sally had called Rob in the car on the way home, I'd overheard him saying, "We are NOT having another dog!" Oops.

Meanwhile at the vet's, Ian took one look at Buddy and shook his head with a melancholy expression on his face. This was as bad as I thought – or maybe even worse. It was clearly the worst case of neglect he'd ever seen too. I waited for the verdict with a heavy heart, worrying over what he was going to say.

As Buddy's legs wouldn't fully support him, I laid him down carefully on the examination table so that Ian could check him over. Luckily, Ian told me, Buddy had no broken bones. But he was riddled with demodectic mange, which was the kind of mange that humans can't catch. The infection had caused the terrible scarring around his face. The mange had eaten away at his skin, and Buddy's weakened immune system meant his body couldn't fight it. Ian warned me that Buddy would need an awful lot of care if he was to survive.

The vet then checked over Buddy's teeth to estimate his

age. It turned out that Buddy wasn't an old dog after all. In fact, he was barely an adult, probably only around one year old. Checking further, Ian told me he didn't reckon Buddy had been involved in dog fights, as he didn't have bite and scratch marks on his body; the scarring around his mouth was simply where he'd been ravaged by mange. That was something positive about the situation we were in, I supposed. The bad news was that he had secondary infections in his skin due to having been left in his own mess for all that time.

I have to admit, I did worry that Buddy was a Staffy, as they seemed to have a bad reputation for being aggressive. But I put that to the back of my mind as I got ready to take him back to the stables. This little chap certainly wasn't likely to be aggressive in the state he was in. I knew that the next 24 hours would be critical. So, armed with what I hoped would be life-saving antibiotics and a special treatment for his skin, we headed home to the stables.

Sally had warned Rob that I would be returning with another rescue project. She assured him that it would be "just temporary" and that Buddy would soon be re-homed. In my mind, of course, the poorly Staffy wasn't going anywhere. Buddy and I were an item now, for as long as he lived. I was going through a break-up when Buddy came into my life, and looking back now it feels as if he'd been sent to give me new focus. I didn't recognise that at the time though, as my only concern was to save him. Suddenly, all those weeks of heartache were forgotten.

I'll never forget that first evening at home with Buddy. I half-filled the big butler's sink in the kitchen with warm water. Then I added a few capfuls of anti-bacterial shampoo and carefully lowered the dog into the sink, trying to make sure that the water didn't frighten him.

My brother had once owned a Staffy, but I really didn't know much about the breed. And I knew nothing at all about Buddy – he was a complete stranger to me – so I was learning all the time what he liked and what made him stressed. It quickly became clear that he didn't enjoy it if he couldn't see me at all times. His little shiny eyes would follow me wherever I went, and his ears seemed to flatten if I looked as if I was going to leave the room. It was as if he never wanted me to leave him again. As I was to discover, his separation anxiety would be a big issue for several years to come.

Using pads of cotton wool for Buddy's eye area and a soft cloth for his coat, I gently bathed away the foul dirt and grime that covered the whole of his body. He placidly sat there, bravely not flinching too much when I moved towards his sore face. I took his lovely soft muzzle in my hand, holding it as gently as I could, and looked him in the eye.

"I'm going to make you all better," I said, as I continued to wash away the crusted dirt from his skin and fur.

Bit by bit, his lovely splodgy brown and black brindle markings became clearer, and the real Buddy started to be revealed. One thing was for certain, he loved having a bath. I wondered if this was possibly the first tender care he'd ever been given. I talked to him the whole time, telling him what a brave boy he was. It broke my heart to think about what he'd been through and how scared he must have been, abandoned in that crate and left to die.

I've always loved dogs. From when I was tiny, it was always my dream to have a Cocker Spaniel with big round expressive eyes and a beautiful soft coat that I could groom every day. I'd never considered owning a Staffy myself, and I'd always thought that they were favoured by people to use as status dogs rather than as lovely pets.

It would never have occurred to me that a solid Bull Terrier like Bill Sikes's dog Bullseye in Oliver Twist was actually as soft as a pussycat. But it was clear that this Staffy I was currently bathing in my kitchen sink was the most gentle creature I'd ever encountered. I wondered if he'd learned to be so passive because he'd been through so much abuse and whether, perhaps, if he ever regained his health, I would see a different character emerge. But at that moment, seeing him so vulnerable and desperate, I couldn't believe he had an aggressive bone in his body.

Cleaning the caked-in dirt from around his claws was a slow process, as Buddy's paw pads were so sensitive. I used several cotton buds to carefully wipe away the almost welded-on grit. The little fellow tensed up if I was too close to the quick of his nails. I was trying to be as gentle but effective as I could, so that afterwards he may be able to sleep and start healing. It took over an hour and several changes of water to get him clean, but my little Buddy was as good as gold throughout the whole thing, bless him.

Once I was satisfied he was clean, I carried him to the kitchen table, wrapped him up in a big fluffy towel to keep him warm and cosy, and patted him dry, being extra careful not to drag or tear any of his sore skin. I then cooked some mini-fillets of chicken and a sachet of rice, and gave him a little plateful of food and a bowl of water. He was a good eater from the start, which was hardly surprising. But I didn't want to give him too much food in case it upset his stomach, as he probably wasn't used to eating much at all. But I knew if he ate something and could keep it down, he would stand a better chance of making it through the night.

I called my best friend, Aunty Pat (you'll hear lots more about her later in the book), and I told her about finding

Buddy. Like all my family, she's a dog lover, and she was horrified when I told her what a poorly state he was in. I said I wasn't sure what I was going to do with him, but for the moment I just wanted to nurse him and try to help him get his strength up. As always, she was very supportive, but she warned me not to get too emotionally attached to him in case everything didn't "go to plan". I think that was her coded way of saying in case he didn't survive. I said I would try not to, but I think I'd fallen in love with him already, to be honest. Those pitiful eyes told me that I really was his last hope. So I knew I had to do my best for him.

I found a big plastic box, left over from when I'd first moved into my home. I thought this would make a good makeshift dog bed. I put a blanket in the bottom of it, then one of my pillows, and finally my favourite soft blue wool scarf. I gently lay Buddy on top and placed it right next to my bed where I could watch him easily during the night. I brushed my teeth, put my pyjamas on and climbed into bed. Buddy and I lay there, looking at one another. I wondered what he was thinking. It had certainly been one of the most unusual days of my life.

I suppose mums with newborns have similar nights where they can't help checking whether their baby is still breathing, watching out for any signs of distress. I felt like that with Buddy, as if I was awake most of the night checking in on him, longing for him to be okay. Halfway through the night, he seemed so lifeless that I really didn't think he was going to make it. He was so floppy as I picked him up and gently held him to me so that he could feel my warmth. Once again, his breathing was almost non-existent. It was heartbreaking.

Please, no, I thought. Don't go. I could feel tears welling up in my eyes. All the emotion that had been building up inside me, first with those two poor foals and then with Buddy, became too much. I already felt such a connection with him and I couldn't bear the idea that I could lose him. I couldn't stop thinking that if I'd found him just a day or two sooner, he might have had a better chance. Eventually I couldn't stop the tears from falling, and I cried and cried for the first time that day.

I started bargaining with the universe. If you let him live, I'll never complain again. If you let him live, I'll do more charity work... My mind was a frenzy of possible scenarios. As the hours ticked by, I felt less and less confident that fate would be on my side. Buddy seemed to be sound asleep one minute, then would jerk awake the next and let out a little whimper in pain. It was terrible to see and distressing to hear.

I guess that at some stage I must have drifted off to sleep, as the next thing I remember is hearing the birds singing, the stables coming to life and the light seeping through the curtains. Coming to my senses, I turned to face Buddy and found that he was looking up at me. It was as if he was saying, "I'm here for you, too. We're going to be okay."

"This is it," I told him, gazing at that little scarred face with those thoughtful eyes. "This is us."

Buddy gets settled

As I climbed out of bed that morning, I wouldn't say Buddy was exactly smiling, but he definitely seemed a lot perkier. I'm sure he nodded when I asked him if he would like some breakfast (okay, I may have made that bit up).

Ian the vet had suggested that I try feeding Buddy some scrambled eggs, and they went down a treat. Watching him happily gobble up the eggs, the sun shining through the windows, I smiled, thinking about how much I was looking forward to spending my first proper day with my new best buddy. Even though Buddy was only a teeny bit better than he'd been the night before, it was something to be positive about.

I had some holiday owed to me from my job at the job

centre, so I called in to say that I wouldn't be in for the rest of the week. I knew I wouldn't be leaving them in the lurch or anything, as I had quite a junior role at the time. Although I was feeling overtired and emotionally drained, my entire focus was on Buddy. I remember thinking that I could catch up on all my sleep once I knew he was out of the woods.

I figured that fresh, warm air would do us both some good. So I took out the picnic blanket and laid it out on the grass near the stables. As Buddy's skin was so sensitive, I made sure he wasn't in direct sunlight, choosing a spot that also wasn't too shady so he could still feel warm and cosy. I know from personal experience that it's always lovely to feel the heat on your bones when you're cold and achy.

Every now and then, Buddy would try to stand up and walk towards me like a wobbly Bambi, but his back legs were too weak to support him. He would lean back constantly and then fall onto his bottom. I could tell he was in the most terrible pain as he seemed restless, with a doleful expression in his eyes. His paws seemed to be causing him the most agony – he kept trying to move them but then giving up, and he was even too weak to bark or whine in distress.

Then I had a brainwave. I quickly popped to the local Asda down the road to buy a couple of pairs of baby socks. When I came back home, I padded the soles of the socks with cotton wool. I figured that in the same way poultices work for horses, the socks would help to cushion poor Buddy's sore paw pads. He barely had the strength to stand up, but I wanted to help him build up his confidence if he tried again – I was worried that he wouldn't otherwise try at all. Sure, the socks looked a little bit silly on him – especially as they were way too big and I had to keep them on with sticky tape – but I thought it was worth a go. The next time he wobbled onto his feet, he managed to stay upright for a few more seconds. It was a step in the right direction anyway.

I caught up with Sally and Rob to get the lowdown on the new foals, and told them all about Buddy's first night. They thought he looked much better – and smelled better too. He was certainly a lot more fragrant than the first time they'd met.

The issue of what was eventually going to happen to him was a real elephant in the room. It was so obvious that we should be talking about this, and also about whether I would be taking him to one of the local rescue centres. But I just couldn't bring up the topic. For the time being, it was a matter of giving Buddy plenty of TLC at the stables until he was fit enough to move on – and I felt that I was the best person to help as we seemed to have bonded. One step at a time, I told myself.

We made it through the day with me hand-feeding Buddy more chicken and rice – he enthusiastically wolfed down everything I offered him – and then I bathed him again that night to get more of the mange treatment into his pores. He looked up at me as I gently sponged him with warm water, and I told him what a good boy he was. Never once did he look irritated or snarl at me, even though his poor little body was obviously really sore.

Later that evening, I turned on my laptop and did some research on Staffordshire Bull Terriers. Reading the Kennel Club's website, the first thing I discovered was that the breed shares the same ancestry as the Bull Terrier – it's a Bulldog crossed with the Black and Tan Terrier. The Staffy was originally developed in the Black Country (in Staffordshire and northern parts of Birmingham) as a fighting dog during the 19th century.

I worried at first about Buddy's temperament – that what I was seeing now wouldn't be the full picture once he was well again. I was reassured to read that despite the breed's origins, Staffies are actually a lot softer than their fearsome reputation would have you believe. In fact, their kind and patient temperament means that they're great with children – so much so, in fact, that they're nicknamed "the nanny dog". The idea that they're aggressive by nature is completely unfounded, and Staffies are considered to be great family pets.

I was also pleased to learn that they have big personalities. As I was to discover firsthand over the coming months, Staffies are boisterous, fun-loving and hugely affectionate dogs. They're far happier running around and playing than acting tough. Since they have so much energy, they need up to an hour's exercise every day. Looking at Buddy in his pitiful state, I couldn't imagine him running around anywhere, but I was determined to try to make that happen.

Staffies are generally robust and hardy dogs, but Ian had warned me that Buddy's progress was likely to be slow. There was a chance that he may never be a "normal" dog who was able to go on walks or interact with strangers. Worse still, Ian told me that I needed to be realistic about Buddy's chances of survival. It would be touch and go for a while. I later found out that Ian had written "Prognosis is guarded" on Buddy's medical notes – in other words, he didn't reckon his prospects were remotely good.

Ian wasn't the only one with concerns. Whenever any of the stable hands saw him or anyone else who was visiting, they'd audibly wince and shake their heads. A few days later, my cousin came round to see Buddy, took one look at him, and said, "That dog needs putting down!" I was so upset. But, if anything, it just made me more determined to do absolutely everything I could for Buddy.

None of my family and friends were the slightest bit surprised when I told them what I'd done. They all knew how much I loved animals. When I told my brother Steven that I'd rescued a dying dog, knowing my love of animals; he just said, "Of course you did…"

One of my earliest memories as a little girl was when I found a sorry-looking old cat in our back garden and I hid him in the garden shed. I would steal bits of food for him from the kitchen and then sneak them out to him and give him lots of cuddles. After a few days, my father saw me sneaking into the shed and discovered what I was up to. He was furious. I know now that I shouldn't have kept the cat in there, but I just couldn't help myself. Luckily, my next-door neighbour said she would look after him for me. We named the cat Tiddles. I suppose he was my first rescue project.

Looking back, I wonder if this may have been my way of giving something the love and affection that I craved for myself. I think that same instinct also kicked in when I saw Buddy. I couldn't bear the idea that he'd been neglected, and I wanted to make amends for the humans who had behaved so appallingly towards him.

On another level, I think I was drawn to help him because I needed help too. Having recently ended a serious relationship, I felt very raw and vulnerable, unwanted and rejected. The moment Buddy looked at me with those pleading eyes, I knew he wanted me as much as I wanted him. In fact, we needed each other. And I was determined to do my very best for him: by healing him, I was healing myself of heartache. It was a fresh new focus that would help me to move on in life. Although I rescued Buddy that day, he'd also rescued me.

Day by day, my little Buddy grew stronger and started to put on weight, but it was a very long, drawn-out process. It took around six weeks of careful bathing and antibiotics for the mange to even begin to clear up. I never gave up hope though. Little by little, Buddy's angry red patches seemed to calm down. His skin became less sensitive and his fur appeared to be growing back where he had been completely bald when I first found him. He started to look perkier too, as if new energy was beginning to flood through his veins.

The raw pink boy I had rescued back in the spring started to sport a summer coat. As I massaged his velvet-soft ears, he would close his eyes in pleasure and wag his tail. He really did seem to be on the mend, but I was still anxious that what he'd been through might end up killing him. By now, I really couldn't bear the idea of life without him.

We already had such a connection. I talked to him all the time about absolutely everything, just chatting away about what I was having for tea, if I needed to do my washing, all that routine stuff that I suppose you may talk to your flatmate about. I would be lying if I said he looked interested, but he did seem to like hearing my voice and knowing that I was around. It's no wonder that he was such an anxious soul after what he'd been through.

I took Buddy to see Ian for regular check-ups over those first few weeks, wanting to make sure that I was doing everything I could to help Buddy get well again. Ian seemed really pleased with the progress that Buddy was making, and he was impressed that I'd been such a good nurse.

Meanwhile, back at the stables, Buddy was beginning to show his real personality. Scamp and Zeus had initially seemed a bit aloof towards the Staffy, but the plucky fellow could certainly hold his own with them. Even though he was still very ill, he had a certain confidence about him, almost as if to say, "Hey, I've been through a lot, this doesn't faze me." He was also great with the horses and seemed to have a real connection with the rescue foals that had been found on the same day as him. We would never know for sure if the man selling the horses had also been Buddy's owner, but there was definitely some kind of rescue-animal kinship between the three creatures.

As time went on, everybody at the stables began to love Buddy as much as I did. But I knew that this didn't mean he was going to be able to live there indefinitely. Every so often, Sally would raise the subject when I was around.

"I think I may have found a home for Buddy. It's so and so from the village," she would say.

Each time she said it, a shiver would run down my spine at the idea that I may have to say goodbye to him. I couldn't see how Buddy would manage to live with anybody else. He would get so frightened if I left him for any longer than a few minutes, sometimes even chewing his paws until they bled. I'd confided in Megan, one of my friends at the stables, that I really wanted to keep Buddy.

"You have to say something to Sally and Rob," she told me. "I don't think they understand how strongly you feel about him."

I didn't know what to do for the best. I was worried Sally and Rob would tell me that Buddy couldn't stay at the stables any longer – and that would mean that I couldn't stay either as I rented a room there. There was no way I was going to be parted from my little Buddy now. *As long as I don't say anything*, I told myself, *we can carry on this lovely life that we have together.*

But there was a problem with my plan. As Buddy

became more confident, the cheeky thing also became more mischievous. It was hardly surprising really. He was nearly an adult dog that had been denied a puppyhood. So he was making up for lost time. This was fine when I was around, as I could keep an eye on him and make sure he didn't get under anyone's feet at the stables. But I needed to make arrangements for when I was back at work in town. Sally had a business to run, and it wouldn't have been fair of me to ask her to keep an eye on him. I needed to come up with a plan – and quick.

Given how much Buddy hated being left alone, I needed to find someone who would be at home all day with him. The most obvious person was my dad. He was retired and lived on my route into work. We'd had a terrible relationship during my childhood. At one stage, he'd have been the last person I'd ever have considered babysitting for my precious Buddy. But I had to do the best I could for Buddy. Besides, I thought this could be the thing that would finally help to mend the broken relationship between me and my dad.

My early years

One of my very earliest childhood memories is being upstairs at our first house. My mum was lying in bed and I was snuggling up to her as she told me I was her special girl. I suppose I must have been about four at the time. Thinking back, as far as I could tell, Mum was always in bed. I didn't really understand why, or even think it was unusual in any way. What I didn't know at the time was that she suffered with chronic migraines that could leave her incapacitated for days, or, as I was to discover much later as an adult, that Dad used to knock her about. It's little wonder that she preferred to try to escape from it all. Luckily though, you never really question things like that when you're very little.

Ours was a very quiet house, considering there were five of us living there: Mum and Dad; my sister Michelle, who was 12 years older than me; my brother Steven, who was 10 years older; and me, the baby of the family. I never found out why there was such a big gap between me and Steven. I guess it was just one of those things.

Weirdly, I can remember more about the design of the house than what was happening inside it: the sunny floral wallpaper in the hallway, the swirly patterned stair carpet and of course the bedroom that I shared with Michelle. I recall being really jealous because Michelle had a cabin bed, whereas mine was just an ordinary little one, like in *Goldilocks and the Three Bears*. I suppose it was a bit strange that two sisters with such a big age difference should end up sharing a room, but it was only a three-bedroom house, so we had no choice, and we rubbed along just fine. I was so tiny in those days that it wasn't like two teens clashing over the space. I was just her little dolly.

I wish I could remember more about that time, as it was to be the only period of my life that I was with my real family. But I can't, as it's all just a vague blur. I was so young, and I think that what came next meant I've spent the rest of my life trying to block out my early childhood. I don't have any family photos from back then either. I guess Mum didn't really want her picture taken, and Michelle and Steven were in that difficult teenage phase, where they'd always run away when the camera came out, so I only have a few sketchy memories of that time. Maybe it's just as well really.

Just before my fifth birthday, Mum died of a brain haemorrhage. I don't remember anything about it, or the funeral itself, just that quite soon afterwards we all moved in with Dad's new girlfriend, Cheryl. Dad told us that we had to behave ourselves at Cheryl's house as she was doing such a lovely thing for us, allowing us all to move in and agreeing to be our new mum.

And that was that, end of discussion. None of us raised any objections. We all just went along with it, but then what choice did we have? In those days, we couldn't just leave home and divorce our parents and do our own thing, as much as we may have liked to.

From the word go, none of us liked Cheryl – and it soon became apparent that the feeling was mutual. To be fair, Cheryl could have been Mother Teresa and it wouldn't have made any difference at the time – she still would never have been able to replace our lovely mum. But Cheryl was far from being Mother Teresa.

She already had two children of her own, and I suppose it's only natural that she cared about them more than she did about us three. Neither of her kids made much attempt to make me feel welcome. Her eldest, Aiden, was five years older than me. I recall him being quite nice to me at first, although later on he used to bully me. His sister Janet, on the other hand, made me feel unwelcome from the moment we moved in. She was two years older than me, and I guess she hated the idea that she may not be the special baby of the house any more.

Not that there was any danger of that. Janet was Cheryl's little princess, and my arrival wasn't going to change that. I vividly recall how they both seemed to really resent my long blonde hair. Cheryl proceeded to let Janet's brown hair grow long and would plait it and tie it in bunches with glittery hair slides and pretty ribbons. I, on the other hand, had to have my hair chopped like a boy's. Every few months, Cheryl would plonk a plastic bowl on my head and cut around it with the kitchen scissors. It looked ridiculous, and I remember people laughing at me afterwards.

A second cousin of mine, who is a hairdresser, reminded me recently that one day she came over and offered to cut my hair, but Cheryl was having none of it. She wanted me to look like a boy and that was that. My cousin refused to cut my hair like that, so it was back to the plastic bowl.

Being so much older, Michelle and Steven soon got the measure of Cheryl, but Dad didn't seem able to see how unhappy we were living at her house. None of us liked it there, yet it felt like he just didn't care. Perhaps he was suffering with unspoken grief of his own, but it made for a pretty miserable life.

When we first moved in, Michelle shared a room with Janet and me. But she couldn't bear it, and it wasn't long before she'd made arrangements to live with my mum's aunt, Pat. That's Aunty Pat, who I've mentioned before. She was really our Great Aunty Pat, but we never called her that. Steven also began to spend as much time as he could at his friends' houses or round at my Nanna's – he moved in with Nanna for good not long after Michelle left. So now it was just Dad, Cheryl, her kids and me.

You'd think with fewer mouths to feed, it may have eased things a bit with Cheryl. If anything though, the tension became worse and I became even more introverted. I remember how Aiden and Janet used to eat their dinner really quickly because they always got what they wanted to eat, like a giant bowl of mashed potatoes. There was no point in complaining, as Cheryl would always give me something she knew I didn't like. I used to have to sit on my own in the kitchen finishing everything on my plate while they would be watching TV in the living room. I'd hide food in a sock and throw it away over the garden wall or dump it in a hedge when we went out.

Those first few years at Cheryl's were awful. For the most part, I tried to keep as quiet as possible and tried to blend in. I really wanted to live with Michelle at Aunty Pat's, but Dad was adamant that I had to stay with him at Cheryl's and that there would be no more picking and choosing where we lived. I know Michelle and Steven both felt bad for leaving me there, but they couldn't cope with the toxic atmosphere at Cheryl's place.

The only really happy memories I have of my early childhood involve my time at infant school, not least because it meant I was apart from Janet, who'd already started junior school. My little school had its own farm area, with a donkey and some sheep that we could stroke and feed, plus a pets' corner so we could learn more about nature. My lovely teacher would encourage everyone to get involved with the animals. I remember earnestly watching tadpoles turning into frogs and bright yellow chickens hatching in the incubator. We were able to hold the animals, and I couldn't believe how precious they were. It really was a magical time. I would always be the first to put my hand up when it came to feeding them or cleaning out the cages. Little did I know that I would be doing an awful lot of mucking out in later life.

The car journeys to infant school every morning felt like a reprieve, an escape from Janet and her horrible bullying. Unfortunately, this proved to be short-lived, as the following year I had to go to the same school as Janet so we travelled together. It felt like I'd been given a prison sentence. I just knew it was going to be hell.

We were supposed to be step-sisters, but Janet would deny we were in any way related and refused to have anything to do with me – other than to bully or belittle me. It was one thing after the other. Early on during my time at the new school, for instance, I had to wear an eye patch for a while to help correct a lazy eye. Janet and her friends would point at me, laugh and make pirate jokes. Day after day, they'd pull my school bag off me, throw it on the floor and kick me in the shins. It felt like I was always covered in bruises. They also used to put chewed-up chewing gum in my hair and in my pockets and laugh at me trying to pick it clean.

I never told anyone about the bullying. I thought that would just make things worse – that Janet would tell Cheryl, who would only punish me even more. My survival tactic was to try to keep myself to myself and not make a fuss, no matter how horrible it became. But this meant I found it harder to make friends.

I was always a loner at school and I constantly felt left behind in every subject. The more I tried to catch up, the more confused I became. Since I had no friends, I could never ask anybody over or go to their houses to play. I never became part of any friendship groups or was invited to birthday parties. When someone in my class came in holding a pile of invitations in their hand, I would think, *Maybe today I'll be invited*. But it just never happened.

After wearing the eye patch for around six months, I was prescribed really ugly National Health glasses which, as expected, Janet and her friends made fun of too. One day at home, Aiden belted me so hard that he sent the glasses flying and they smashed on the patio. Cheryl went berserk and blamed me for annoying him and making him lose his temper, and she sent me straight to bed.

Cheryl would send me to bed at 5.30pm every school night, even when I was nine years old. Lying in bed, I could hear Janet playing with her friends outside in the sunshine. I was still sharing a room with her, and when she came to bed hours later she would make me turn to face the wall so that she could watch the television. I was never allowed to watch it with her. What's more, she would have the volume on so loud that I wouldn't be able to sleep. I would retreat into my own silent bubble and quietly cry. I couldn't even let her see me get upset or she would just call me a cry baby.

It was such a miserable time. Cheryl never treated me like a proper daughter. If I was ever ill, I would have to go straight to bed and wasn't allowed any food. If Janet was poorly, she would be tucked up with a bottle of Lucozade and a tray of eggy soldiers. Cheryl would stroke her hair and place her cuddly toys around her, pretending they were her nurses. I always wished Dad would do that with me, but he never did. One day I remember Janet put some fake blood on my Barbie dolls and told me they'd been murdered. She wasn't just a cruel girl – she was disturbed. Like Cinderella, I thought I had a wicked family and I longed for a happy ending.

If I wasn't being sent to bed, I would be cleaning the bathroom, washing the kitchen floor or hoovering instead. Cheryl was a home help, so she claimed that she never had time to do any cleaning at our house and that I had to do it. Dad, meanwhile, was a jack of all trades – a milkman, a plumber, a bit of work here, a bit of work there... But even though the two of them were always busy, there was never enough money for us to go on holiday – although I'm pretty sure Janet went on every school trip on offer.

I was left on my own a lot. One day, I wrote a letter to Mum in heaven, telling her how unhappy I was and how I wished she was with me. I didn't send it – I didn't know how to – so kept it under my pillow, hoping the fairies would take it to her. Then one day it was gone. I never found out what happened to it. I can't believe Janet took it because I'm sure she would have teased me about it, so I guess it must have been Cheryl. She never mentioned it. Perhaps it pricked at her conscience.

A few months later, when I was eight, my mum's younger brother, Nick, asked me to be a bridesmaid at his wedding. I was thrilled to bits, of course – it's every little girl's dream to wear a pretty bridesmaid's dress and matching shoes. Cheryl said I could do it, but only on the condition that Janet was a bridesmaid too. But that was never going to happen, as Nick had fallen out with Dad and Cheryl for moving in together so quickly after Mum's death.

I was heartbroken about not being a bridesmaid, but Cheryl was adamant. Then my wonderful Aunty Pat did the most thoughtful thing – she made me a special party dress similar to the ones the bridesmaids were wearing, so that I could still feel part of the celebrations. She cleverly made it different enough so that Cheryl wouldn't be able to make a fuss about it and stop me from wearing it.

While I was having a horrible time with the humans in my life, animals became my release. Cheryl used to make me clean out the huge aviary in the back garden, which was quite a big job for a tiny girl. But I loved the birds, and at least they didn't judge me or call me names. I loved Cheryl's two dogs too. She had a little Norfolk Terrier called Alfie and a grey whippet called Lola. I would take them out for walks whenever I could. It was a great way of getting out of the house, and it meant that I wouldn't be picked on for half an hour or so. I would often have to go outside in the rain because nobody else wanted to take the dogs out in bad weather, but I didn't mind. For me, it was an escape.

One day while I was out walking the dogs, Lola cut her paw on a sharp piece of the drain. Her paw started to bleed quite badly, so I gently wrapped it up and carried the dog home, dreading what Cheryl would say about it. Unsurprisingly, she accused me of cutting Lola deliberately. She said I was a cruel and evil child and sent me upstairs to bed. What was even worse was that Dad believed her. I remember sobbing, pleading my innocence, but neither of them would believe me. I keep saying, "Who would ever deliberately hurt an animal?" Back then, it was totally beyond my comprehension.

One year for my birthday, I was given one of Janet's old bikes, one that she'd grown out of. I used to ride to the nearby field so that I could look at the horses there. I would spend as long as I could watching them, and I loved seeing them being ridden by other people around the nearby farm. *One day*, I thought, *I'm going to do that*. Never in a million years did I really ever believe that I would end up having several horses of my very own throughout my life.

Knowing I was so unhappy at Cheryl's, Mum's younger sister, Angie, would often invite me over to stay with her and my cousins Jacqualene, Martin, Kerry and PJ at the weekend. I loved it there. I could do anything I wanted to do. I remember Aunty Angie being really surprised one day when I asked for a glass of water – she couldn't believe that I always had to ask permission for something that basic. She said I should just help myself if I was thirsty. She also couldn't believe that I would always ask if it was okay if I used the loo. The penny was starting to drop about just how badly I was being treated at Cheryl's place.

Week after week, I would cry at the end of the weekend when the time came for me to go back home. I didn't want to tell tales about what was happening at Cheryl's, as I remember Dad telling me that she was doing a very generous thing letting us move in with her. Besides, I never for one minute thought that it would make any difference anyway. I just knew that the life I had at Aunty Angie and Uncle Rick's was a million miles away from the one I had at Cheryl's.

Aunty Angie knew that I loved staying at their place, and finally she intervened and asked if she could legally foster me. It turns out that she had been thinking about it for a long time. When Mum had died six years earlier, her youngest sister, Yvonne, had asked if she could bring me up. But back then, there was never any question of Dad letting me go. That was before two of his other children had voted with their feet. After a few years of living at Cheryl's, even he could see how unhappy I was getting. And although I didn't know it at the time, things weren't exactly perfect between him and Cheryl either.

I can't remember all the ins and outs of that stage of my life. But by the time I reached the age of 11, the legal fostering papers had been signed and I became a proper member of Aunty Angie and Uncle Rick's family. They were so kind to me. I think they wanted to make up for all the unhappy years I'd had before. After that, my life seemed to completely turn around.

For the first time ever, I was properly happy. I loved hanging out with my cousin PJ, who was in the year below me at school. We had a hamster called Monty and each of us had a goldfish that we'd carefully put in the bath while we cleaned out their tanks. Whether or not we got our own fish back at the end of the cleaning session is debatable. But for the first time in my life, I had a pet of my own and also my own things, rather than just sharing Janet's and always having to wear her hand-me-downs.

My brother Steven bought me a desk and chair for my bedroom, which made me feel really grown-up and special.

It was such a lovely thing for him to think of doing for me. Maybe the best thing of all was that I had a bedroom of my own, with my lovely desk and chair inside it, and my posters of Take That, the Backstreet Boys, Boyzone and Blue up on the walls. Every space on the wall was covered with either pop posters or pictures of horses.

I recently read a card that I sent to Angie and Rick when I first moved in with them. Inside it, I'd told them how much I loved living with my new family. It really felt like a totally new life. I'd been accepted as a member of their family, and Jacqualene, Martin, Kerry and PJ were proper brothers and sisters to me. I could run around, go blackberry picking, climb trees, play games and be a proper child. I wasn't sent to bed early. I could have friends to stay and go to their houses for sleepovers.

For me, what was essentially a normal happy childhood for others felt like a hundred birthdays all at once. What's more, I felt like I was allowed to show my feelings for the first time in my life. If I was upset about something, Angie would encourage me to talk it through with her. If I was happy, I wasn't told off for getting "giddy" or "overexcited". That was seen as a crime at Cheryl's place. I don't think I stopped smiling for five years!

Daily life was lovely, but holidays were even better. During my first summer living with Angie and Rick, we spent a magical week in Chapel St Leonard in Lincolnshire. Angie and Rick would hire a chalet there every year; Martin had cerebral palsy and was in a wheelchair, so other kinds of holidays weren't really suitable. We all loved it there and had a great time, making sandcastles, playing games and being out in the fresh air all day.

One day, while the others were off getting ice creams and cups of tea, I asked Martin if he would like to be closer to the sea. He said yes straight away. So off I went, pushing his wheelchair down the beach. Trouble was, I pushed it too far and the wheels became stuck in the sand. The more I tried to move it, the more stuck it became.

As the waves started to get closer, Martin burst out laughing. He thought it was the funniest thing ever, but I was terrified and went into a blind panic as I remembered how I'd been punished before. I begged Martin not to tell Angie and Rick what I'd done, but that only made him laugh even more. Luckily, a kind passerby saw what was going on and yanked the wheelchair out of the sand and back on to a more solid bit of the beach, so I could take Martin to where we were meant to be. I've actually never admitted that before. I hope I'm not in trouble!

My first proper Christmas together with my new family was wonderful, with everyone eating far too many Quality Street and drowning in a sea of wrapping paper. Angie and

Rick had bought me and PJ new mountain bikes; mine was a deep metallic pink and I loved it. I'd never before been given such a generous gift that was new – and all mine. The other really fantastic thing about that Christmas Day was not being forced to stay at the table until I'd eaten absolutely everything on my plate – for the first time ever in my life, I could leave the sprouts. That afternoon, as PJ and I zoomed around the streets on our new bikes, I don't think I'd ever been happier.

Discovering my love of horses

Shortly after I moved into Angie and Rick's place in 1995, another cousin of mine, Leanne, started having riding lessons at a nearby equestrian centre. Knowing how crazy I was about horses, Leanne's mum Yvonne had a word with the centre's owners, Sally and Rob. She asked them if I could go along too, to help out. Thankfully, they said yes. This place would end up becoming a major part of my life, and the reason that I would one day meet Buddy.

It was wonderful there. As well as Sally's beautiful horses, there were cats, dogs, rabbits, ducks and geese. I loved it. There was always so much for me to do. One minute I would be mucking out and haying the horses, the next I would be cleaning out the rabbit hutches and walking the dogs, or picking up the poo from the fields (it's a dirty job, but someone has to do it). I never minded what I did. I would do anything if it meant I could hang out at the stables.

It wasn't long before I became a regular member of the team. I would be there pretty much every weekend and whenever I possibly could during my school holidays. My brother Steven, would drop me off on his way into work so that I could be there first thing to give the horses their breakfast, and then I would stay all day. I was in heaven.

I made a new friend there, called Heather. She was as mad about horses as I was, and we spent a lot of time together as stable hands. We were able to exercise the horses and I quickly learned how to ride properly. I was determined to master the riding, although I must admit that it took a fair bit of practice for me get the rhythm right with trotting. I would often end up with a numb bum when I first started, but it never put me off. When you really want to do something, you put your "all" into it.

After a while, I was given a horse on half-loan. This meant that I had my "own" horse on the days I was at the equestrian centre. It was my responsibility to exercise the horse, make sure it was fed and hydrated and muck out its stables. There was no way I could ever have afforded my own horse at the time, so this was a fabulous opportunity.

Much as I loved life at the stables, there were sad times too. No matter how well you care for an animal, it's inevitable that some will get ill or, even worse, pass away. Heather and I learned the harsh reality of this one day when we were out feeding the horses.

I was 14 at the time. We'd gone to hay the horses in a field. We had to supplement their feed, as there wasn't enough goodness in the grass they were grazing on. We would heave great big bags of hay into the field and then call the horses down to us. In the past, this had always prompted them to come running, which was always thrilling to see. But on this day, although there were around a dozen horses to be called in, only a couple of them came over to us.

We went to investigate what was going on, heading back to the field where the two horses had run from. We were horrified to discover that a beautiful ex-racehorse called Molly had broken her leg. The lower part of her leg was actually dangling loosely from her knee. It was a real shock.

Meanwhile, the other horses were all standing around her in a circle, in some kind of show of sympathy I guess, almost as if they were keeping guard. Heather and I were both really upset and ran straight back to the stables to get Sally. We didn't want to make a fuss as she was busy with something else at the time. But, without thinking, I heard myself blurt out, "Molly's broken her leg... and it's hanging off!"

While Sally called the vet and made her way to the field, Heather and I ran ahead. It was a bitterly cold day, but we took off our coats and laid them over Molly to try to keep her warm and calm. We both sensed there was nothing that could be done and that Molly would have to be destroyed. We knew enough about horses at this point to know that this kind of injury couldn't be cured. I felt so helpless. It was my first experience of seeing an animal in so much distress, and I just couldn't bear it.

Back then, euthanised horses were shot rather than being put to sleep by injection. There was no way I could possibly watch that. As soon as I realised what was going to happen, I ran off, with my hands over my ears so that I didn't have to hear the gunshot. It was impossible to tell exactly how Molly had been injured, but the hunt had been through the field that day and Sally wondered if maybe Molly had tried to gallop with them, breaking her leg in the process.

Whatever the reason, the outcome was the same, and Heather and I were utterly heartbroken. I remember going back to stay at Heather's house that night and the two of us were in floods of tears, not just for Molly, but for our own horses. What would happen when they died? My loan pony was a very elderly dark bay called Bella. I couldn't bear to think of ever having to say goodbye to her.

When that time did come, a couple of years later, I was at school. My beloved Bella was put to sleep by injection. Sally called Angie with the news, and Angie told me when I arrived home. I was absolutely devastated. It felt as if my heart was actually broken. I felt physical pain without her and couldn't eat a thing. I was in such a bad way.

Grieving for an animal somehow feels more raw than grieving for a person. You feel their life is in your hands, from what you feed them and how you keep on top of any health changes to the environment they live in and the exercise they get. You care for an animal every day of its life and make every single decision for it.

Saying goodbye to any of the horses at the stables was always hard, but the happy times I spent there far outweighed the sad. As you may have gathered, I was horse mad as a kid. From the age of about 12, I would go on riding school holidays to Thetford Forest in Suffolk that Sally organised. Around 20 children would attend, and we'd all stay in static caravans and have great adventures – pony trekking, boating, bowling, going out to the cinema and generally having a magical time. Angie and Rick would pay a little towards it, but it was an expensive trip. I think I was mostly there because of Sally and Rob's generosity.

I thought I was luckier than the other children as I used to have a caravan to myself. I shared this with Rob and Sally's two dogs, a rescue greyhound called Storm and a rescue lurcher called Gemma. Both dogs were rather highly strung and didn't like having any of the other kids near them. Storm would growl at the other children, but not at me for some reason, and I felt very grown-up with just the two of them. Trouble was, Storm and Gemma would always take over the bed, so I would end up on the floor. I didn't mind though, as it was all part of the adventure.

Sally has always been wonderful to me. She has been a true friend. When I later went to work for her, she was more like a second mum than a boss. One day when I was over at the stables helping out, she took me with her to a livestock auction at Melton Mowbray. We'd gone to just have a look and not bid on any animals. She had not planned to buy anything, but she ended up falling in love with an Appaloosa horse called Snowflake.

Snowflake was a real beauty, covered in quirky muddy patches, and before I knew it, she was coming home with us. But as we quickly discovered when we took her back to the stables, Snowflake was very nervous around other horses. She seemed to prefer the company of humans – in particular, me. No matter how much we tried to settle her in, she was forever barging through the gate in the field if she thought we were leaving her.

We'd been hoping that she would be one of the horses coming with us on the annual pony trekking holiday to Thetford. But to our surprise, it turned out that she was in foal – which may explain why she'd been so nervous around other horses. Six months later, her foal was born. We named her Snowdrop, and she was every bit as beautiful as her mum. The two of them were just perfect together.

Horses became my passion. I hated school because I was bullied there and quite early on I decided that I wanted to leave when I was 16 and work full-time at a stables. I enjoyed certain subjects such as science and English. Like Steven, I also seemed to have an aptitude for IT, but studying wasn't really my thing.

During the five years I lived with Angie and Rick, I didn't once meet up with Dad. Angie would encourage me to give him a ring every now and then, and I suppose I thought enough of him to try to keep in touch. But I never really had the impression that the feeling was mutual. He never even sent me a birthday card. With hindsight, I suppose I should have been sad about that, but I was too busy loving my life with my new family. Dad would occasionally ring me back if I called him, but he never seemed all that bothered about not being around to see me grow up.

"Oh, I came round to the house earlier, but you weren't there," he would tell me, knowing full well that I would have been at school at the time. "I'll try again another time..."

He never did. But I refused to allow myself to get upset about it. I had a great relationship with Rick, so I never felt that I was missing out on a father figure. Rick was more of a dad to me than my real father had ever been.

Life at the stables

As I'd always planned, I left school when I was 16, after taking my GCSEs. I was determined to start earning money and stand on my own two feet, rather than rely on Angie and Rick to support me. Happily, I didn't have to wait long for an opportunity to come up. A girl at the stables was moving on, so it meant that not only was there a job vacancy, but her room was available.

I couldn't believe my luck: it meant that I could be around horses all day, every day. I wished I could have turned back time and told my nine-year-old self that one day I would be doing my dream job, working at a stables, and living there too.

My excitement about moving to the stables was tinged

with a little sadness though, as it meant I would be leaving Angie and Rick's, and that I would no longer be able to spend as much time with all my cousins there. I knew I would really miss them when I moved out, but it was time for me to begin the next chapter of my life.

Sally and Rob's home at the stables was gorgeous – a former coach house made from red bricks and surrounded by green fields. It was perfect for me, homely and comfortable. I was given a lovely big room that looked out over the fields where the horses grazed. Not only could I see Snowflake and Snowdrop from my bedroom window, but I could be out there with them in the field within minutes of getting up.

Snowflake was now my loan pony. Living at the stables meant I could properly look after her, from mucking out and feeding her to exercising and grooming her and putting her to bed at night. It could be hard work, especially in the winter months when the rain was lashing down and it was extra muddy, but there was no place on earth I would rather have been.

Living at Angie and Rick's had been wonderful, but now I felt like a proper adult, with a proper role to play. From my very first day there as a horse-mad teenager, to my Saturday job as a stable hand and now working there full-time, I'd learned so much about horses and how Sally and Rob's various businesses worked. Every day was full on, and I loved it. There was always something that needed to be done, but I was always made to feel like one of the family. I ate my meals with them every day and they really looked after me.

Most days, I would be up and out no later than seven o'clock in the morning. My first job would be to feed the horses and hang up the hay nets in the stables. The outdoor horses in the fields would also need feeding. I would go around each of the paddocks, taking the horses food, grooming them and giving them some attention. Then I would head back to the stables to swap the horses' rugs to their waterproof outdoor rugs, ready for them to be turned out for the day.

The horses didn't all go in the same place. Some would go to one particular field with certain friends, and others would go to another field with other horses. It depended on which horses could get on well with one another, a bit like human interactions. It sounds complicated, but it was all quite straightforward once you got the hang of it. Then, once all of the horses were out in the fresh air, I would start mucking out the stables, changing hay nets if necessary, giving them fresh water and making up their feeds: one for night-time, and one for the following day. This helped to keep the stable clean and keep the horses healthy.

After that, it would be time to sweep the yard, sort out my own tack (equipment such as my saddle) and, depending on which time of year it was, think about getting the horses back in for the evening. Then I had to swap back the outdoor rugs for the indoor ones, feed the horses and do any other jobs that needed doing. Sometimes I would also help out at the riding school if they were taking the horses out for a hack in the countryside. A hack is when you take a horse for a light ride on and off the roads – it exercises the horse, gives them confidence, provides a change of scenery and helps them unwind. I loved hacking, as it was a chance to take the horses out and about and get to know them better. There was never any shortage of work at the stables, that's for sure. It was all quite physical, but I really enjoyed it.

Sally and I had a great relationship. Because I'd been coming to the stables since I was 11, she knew she could trust me with any of the horses and I never had a problem with the "difficult" ones. These horses would throw off their riders or get a bit feisty if you got too close. I didn't mind though, as I loved their spirit and personality. I had my fair share of tumbles, but I never broke any bones and I always saw experiences like that as part of the learning curve anyway. On one occasion when I was thrown off a horse, it seemed quite bad as I landed heavily on concrete.

But the adrenaline meant that I picked myself up and climbed back on the horse – literally. I was fearless!

I often accompanied Sally on her buying trips. I found it fascinating to go to auctions and watch how the tension would build as the prices rose higher and higher. It wasn't long before I was able to convert a price in guineas to its sterling equivalent. Sometimes, of course, a buying trip would turn out to be more like a mercy mission, like that fateful Monday in April 2009 when I came back with Buddy.

On another trip, Sally and I went to London to buy a Hackney horse, not for the riding school or to loan out, but for Sally to ride herself. The horse she chose, a magnificent mare called Lulu, was an absolute beauty. She was over 16 hands high. Sally knew she was "the one" the moment she set eyes on her. I fell in love with Lulu too. When we returned to the stables, I started to treat her like my own, grooming her and riding her around the fields. Sally could see how much I loved her and very generously let me have her on loan. It was yet another example of how incredibly generous Sally is. Even though she loved that horse, she let me have her. She really is one in a million.

While I loved riding Lulu, my ultimate dream was to buy my own Hackney horse, but it would be a while before I could do that. The first horse I actually bought and paid for myself was a New Forest pony called Zara. I bought her in 2005. The plan was that I would "back" her – in other words, train her up so she would accept a rider on her back – then sell her on with a view to buying my own Hackney horse and carriage. Although New Forest ponies are technically "wild" as they're free to roam the land, they're owned by the various landowners. That means that some will be broken in enough to be easily trained and others will be more of a challenge. I'd always enjoyed a challenge though, so I couldn't wait to get started.

I loved Zara, but I'd set my heart on owning a Hackney ever since Sally had bought Lulu. Hackneys are such handsome, solid horses. The trouble was that vet bills, feed and livery didn't come cheap, and I didn't end up making anywhere near enough money selling Zara to buy my own Hackney. Thankfully, my brother Steven stepped in, as he has done on so many occasions, and loaned me some money to buy my own carriage horse. I think this is where he was first given the nickname "The Bank of Steven". What a hero!

Hackneys can be quite hard to come by – and sadly, they aren't all kept in the best conditions. My friend Sally and I once went to see a dealer with a view to buying a Hackney. When we arrived, we couldn't believe the state his poor horses were in. All of them were really underweight and looked so depressed.

Over the years I've lived in the countryside, I've encountered people who see their animals as a way to make a living rather than creatures to treasure. So this means I've had to really toughen up, yet it doesn't make it any easier. Some owners treat their horses like old cars; they don't see why they need to care for them. If I could, I would have bought the whole lot right there and then.

Happily though, not long after that, I received a call from a trainer in Sutton Coldfield, who told me about a couple with a Hackney they wanted to sell. As soon as I saw the horse's head over the stable door, I was smitten. Matilda was a 15.1 dark bay, with a full white face and white socks. I knew there and then that I had to have her. The owners told me she was quite naughty, but I wasn't bothered. I soon got the measure of her when I brought her back to the stables.

Matilda was a fantastic worker. She would do anything I asked of her – pulling a carriage, going for a hack in the countryside, tackling jumps... Anything. Unfortunately though, she was trouble, just as I'd been warned. She wouldn't tolerate anyone but me changing her rug in the morning, and she could only cope with one person doing something to her at a time or she would start kicking out or biting. Sometimes she would just kick out at you as you walked past for no reason.

Unfortunately, she took against Rob the very first time she saw him. He went up to stroke her and she lunged at him, lifting him up by his chest. It was really scary, and I felt terrible about it. There were no broken bones or bite marks, thank God, but that was the last time Rob went anywhere near her.

As well as owning the stables, Sally and Rob also had a wedding carriage business and I used to help out as one of their grooms. I loved seeing a bride's reaction when we turned up with the carriage to take her to the wedding. I secretly hoped that I would have a horse and carriage on my own special day if I ever married.

It was a lovely, happy business to be involved in, but it was hard work. As well as making sure the horses are beautifully groomed, fit and healthy, the carriage also has to look perfect. It's going to appear in a lot of photos, after all. And then there's your own uniform. It has to be immaculate at all times, from your shirt and starched stock to your jacket, jodhpurs and polished boots. As you may expect, wearing all that gear all day in the middle of summer when it's really hot can be a job in itself.

I know this is going to sound crazy, given that horses had always been my passion, but after a couple of years working at the stables I started to have a re-think about my working life. Work was always busy, which was never a problem. But what had been a hobby for me was now turning into a chore, and I didn't have as much time to spend with my own horses as I would have liked. I didn't feel that I could give them as much attention as I wanted to, as I had to look after the other horses too. Added to that, the stables were in the middle of nowhere and I felt I was missing out a bit when friends told me what they'd been up to. I loved my life at the stables, but I had to admit to myself that I felt a bit stuck. I thought I should try to get a nine-to-five job, so that I could fall in love with my hobby again.

In 2003, I decided to give up my job at the stables. I moved in with Aunty Pat, who'd taken in Michelle after we moved to Cheryl's with Dad. Then I found what I thought was a "sensible" job for the Department of Work and Pensions at the job centre in Leicester. My first role there was as an admin assistant working in data management. It wasn't very taxing. It basically involved going through boxes and doing A LOT of shredding, but the salary was okay and it suited me at the time. I worked hard, but I never saw the job as something I would be doing for long. Little did I know that 16 years later I would still be working there but in a totally different role.

Reuniting with Dad

At around this time in my life, I started to have more contact with Dad. Up until now I hadn't felt inclined to see him – he was hardly father of the year, after all – but the rest of my family had encouraged me to reach out to him, telling me it had been a difficult time for all of us when Mum died and that it was time to put the past behind us. They said I would regret it if we never gave our relationship a chance. I would like to say that meeting up with him again for the first time in more than seven years was a beautiful, emotional moment. But it wasn't. Far from it.

Dad had recently split up with Cheryl. It transpired that she'd got her claws into another man and had kicked Dad out. I don't know the ins and outs of what happened.

But quite honestly, I wasn't especially interested in finding out. I was just glad that this chapter of our lives could be consigned to history. A little part of me felt vindicated that Cheryl wasn't the lovely warm woman that Dad had always tried to persuade us she was, but there was no point in recriminations.

Dad and Michelle hadn't kept in touch over the years either and, like me, she'd never been a big fan of Cheryl. Dad was now staying with Michelle's neighbour and, one night after working at the job centre, I happened to be over at her house when, out of the blue, he appeared in the kitchen.

"Oh, hello," he said.

I'd always said I wasn't bothered about having anything to do with him – but anyway, there he was. It was hardly the most memorable of reintroductions, but then Dad was never exactly one for big displays of emotion. I hadn't seen him for more than seven years and at that moment I felt absolutely nothing for him. I just remember thinking how haggard he looked, so tired and lined from smoking so heavily. Friends have said to me that they're surprised I didn't lose my temper and lay into him about what he and Cheryl had put me through as a child. I'd certainly had enough of those conversations in my head over the years, but instead we just started to make small talk.

I wasn't about to start raking over old ground – whatever I said to him wasn't going to change what had happened in the past – but then he brought up the subject himself. I was gobsmacked. He proceeded to tell me that he'd felt abandoned when Mum had died. I couldn't believe how bitter he was about being left with three children, as if Mum had planned it that way. It was ridiculous. It was if he was trying to justify to me why he moved in with Cheryl so soon after Mum died – that somehow he'd done it for our sakes.

Did he really think I should feel sorry for him? He obviously hadn't been touched by any kind of guilt about how he'd behaved with the three of us. He seemed to think everything had been fine at Cheryl's, even though Michelle and Steven had moved out so soon after, and I was clearly unhappy all the time.

He didn't know the first thing about bonding with his family. By this stage, Michelle had children of her own, but Dad had never had any kind of relationship with his grandchildren. Then again, why would he when he'd hardly bothered with his own children for all those years? It was weird, because he knew how it felt to be rejected, and yet he seemed to be turning down the chance of forming a bond with the next generation.

As I was to discover though, Dad was very ill. He'd

recently been diagnosed with lymphoma and the aggressive chemo and radiotherapy treatment had triggered heart troubles. He'd needed a stem cell transplant and he was now in a really sorry state. He needed his family and, no matter what had gone on in the past between us, I understood that his children needed to be there for him. When all's said and done, you only get one dad, don't you? I was wary, but I wanted to do right by him. Whatever had happened in the past, I had to leave it there and show him that I could be the bigger person. I was an adult now.

After that first meeting, I started to see Dad more regularly, but it was never going to be the kind of father-daughter relationship that my friends had with their parents. We'd never do things like go to the pub together or have a laugh about happy times when I was growing up. It was quite a matter-of-fact relationship. We'd get on, be civil to one another, but we never had a big heart-to-heart about what had gone on when I was little.

In hindsight, I'm pleased that he came back into my life, but at the time it didn't seem to be a big deal. I expect we would have carried on as we were if it hadn't been for finding Buddy. On that day in April 2009, my whole life changed – and not long afterwards so would my relationship with my dad. Who would have thought that a little dog with a bad case of mange would end up bringing us back together?

I was with Sally on the day I found Buddy because by then I'd moved back to the stables, as Aunty Pat needed her spare room for her son. It was good to be back in my room, but I wanted to keep things easy for Sally and Rob, as I wasn't working there any more. I'd started taking my washing round to Dad's house, to do it there rather than at the stables, and in return I would do bits of shopping for him.

Dad loved dogs and had one of his own, a Jack Russell cross called Holly. So he was keen to meet Buddy and kindly offered to mind him while I was out at work. When he suggested it, I think he knew that it would be a way to win back serious Brownie points with me. And it did. Looking after Buddy also gave Dad a new purpose and, just as I'd discovered, it meant he had less time to dwell on his own problems. It was like a kind of mutual pet therapy.

To start with, things worked out really well, as Buddy was still so poorly and would sleep for most of the day, dosed up on painkillers and antibiotics. I would drop him off at Dad's place on the way to work, leave my car there and then catch the bus to and from the job centre. Dad just had to keep an eye on Buddy and reassure him that he wasn't on his own.

Buddy's mange was starting to clear up and, little by

73

little, he was putting on weight, but he still had a long way to go. He was also still wearing the children's socks to cushion his paw pads while they toughened up, and to stop himself from scratching. It would be a long while yet before he resembled a healthy chunky Staffy, but life was looking much more positive for him.

It helped that Buddy and Holly got on really well. Holly would mother Buddy, cleaning him and looking after him. It really was an ideal arrangement, and I've no doubt that it played a big part in healing the rift between me and Dad.

All was fine for the first month or so. But as Buddy gradually grew stronger, I couldn't help worrying that maybe Dad had bitten off more than he could chew. Let's put it this way, Buddy wasn't exactly the perfect houseguest. The first time Buddy "mistook" one of Dad's shoes for his dog chews was quite funny, and to be fair to Dad, he took it in good humour. The second and third times he found less amusing though, especially as Buddy took it upon himself to destroy a different pair each time.

"I wouldn't mind if he took me old shoes that I don't like," Dad complained, "but those are the only ones I wear. Well, at least I *used* to wear them."

Another time, while I was on the bus back to Dad's place to pick up Buddy after work, he phoned me.

"Nicola, can you pick me up some toilet rolls on your

way home, please."

As I looked out of the bus window, I wondered if Dad was losing his mind. "Dad, they're in the cupboard. I bought you a big pack only the other day."

"Well, yes, I know you did, but they seem to be Buddy's new toy."

I shook my head in disbelief. "Oh God, what's happened now?"

"Well, I was having a little sleep this afternoon and somehow he discovered a toilet roll could fit quite nicely through the cat flap, so he decided to take one out into the garden – and shred it. Then he took another. And another. And another. And…"

"Yes, okay, I get it. How many did he destroy?"

Dad paused for a moment. "All of them. An entire 24-pack. I ended up having to hoover the garden."

"Oops. Sorry, Dad…"

At least all of these antics proved that my little Buddy was getting stronger. He was getting a lot more energetic too. If the weather was bad and Dad had kept him indoors all day, Buddy would start to get a bit stir crazy. He devised his own little agility run. He would jump up on a chair, then dive on to the settee and run along the back of it, then jump on to another chair and back round again. He would do this several times a day, as if he was trying to get his

10,000 steps done. He thought it was the best game ever.

Buddy seemed to be on a one-dog mission to destroy Dad's house, but Dad didn't seem at all bothered and would just laugh about it. He'd certainly softened in his old age. One day I came back to Dad's after work and I wrote a letter from Buddy to Steven. It said: "Dear Uncle Steven, my name is Buddy. I know we haven't met yet, but I'm afraid to say I have something I need to tell you: I got a bit hungry and I have just eaten your furniture."

Steven had been storing his garden furniture at Dad's house. Buddy had chewed a hole in his wooden table and taken a chunk out of one of the chairs. Luckily, because Steven is so easygoing, he didn't mind. It's a good job I have such understanding relatives.

Our little routine seemed to be working, with Buddy happily going to Dad's doggy day care and me going off to work. After a while, Buddy had the added bonus that Aunty Pat had moved into the bungalow next door to Dad, so he could see her every day too. At the end of the garden was a gate, and Buddy could choose which direction to take – one way to Aunty Pat's and the other way to Dad's. This provided him with even more cuddle opportunities. What a lucky boy!

I'll never forget Buddy's first Christmas with me. Thinking about it, it was probably his first-ever Christmas as I'm pretty sure every day was just the same for him in his old life. I'd woken up early to feed the horses and was looking forward to spending the day at Aunty Pat's with the family. I knew it was going to be a great day. Like every special occasion, Pat would always go out of her way to make the day fantastic for everyone. She would even make up trays of Christmas dinner for her neighbours and send them round if they were likely to be alone.

At Buddy's first Christmas, he had a lovely pile of presents to open. It was just daft stuff like plastic dog toys and treats. But he tore into them like a Tasmanian devil and ran around in circles with excitement. It was hilarious. My little dog seemed finally to be living his best life.

I wasn't going out with anyone at the time, but hadn't felt alone at all, as I was so unconditionally loved by my little ball of energy. I felt so happy for the first Christmas in years. I'd spent so long with various loser boyfriends and shed too many tears when relationships had failed. But now I had a fantastic new companion, and I knew he'd be there for me through thick and thin.

Buddy goes back to the stables

While Buddy was starting to get healthier, Dad in turn was getting more poorly. I'd come to realise that it wasn't reasonable to expect him to look after Buddy all day. Buddy may have been a fully-grown dog, but at heart he was a great big puppy who wanted to make up for lost time. He seemed to have endless reserves of energy. It was endearing to watch, but exhausting for Dad to have to cope with every day.

When Buddy first arrived in my life, when he was still really sick, it had been tricky to let him run free at the stables. Now that he was hale and hearty though, things were different. Sally was happy to have him around during the day. She said it would be fine for me to leave Buddy there to hang out with the other dogs, not to mention his biggest fan at the stables, Sally's mum Phyllis.

Phyllis, or Gran as we all used to call her as she was Sally's kids' gran, lived in an annexe and quickly became firm friends with Buddy. She would open her front door and call out to him each morning, and off he would trot to see her, wagging his tail. Her own dog, a little Springer-Cocker-cross called Sammy, wasn't especially thrilled about this new arrangement. Sammy didn't have much time for Buddy and would scarper out of the door as soon as Buddy ambled in from the back for his fuss.

Buddy loved Gran, and the two of them would snuggle up on her sofa in front of the fire. She would give him his lunch and then they would sit together for ages and watch recordings of *Downton Abbey* – she said it was their favourite programme. It was so lovely to see him building up his trust with people. If I was now Buddy's mum, Gran was most definitely his new best friend.

Then something extraordinary started to happen. When Buddy went to see Gran each morning, we noticed he would be very clingy with her and refuse to leave her, following her everywhere and getting stressed if she ever left his sight. He'd always been in and out of her place as the mood took him, checking out what was going on outside in the yard, but now he insisted on sticking by her side and was ultra-affectionate. Then, an hour or so later, things would go back to normal and Buddy would once again be in and out of Gran's annexe as he pleased.

We couldn't understand why he was behaving this way, but eventually Gran reckoned she'd worked out why. She was diabetic and had noticed that Buddy would always stay close to her until she'd taken her insulin medication. Once she'd done that, he would be happy to toddle back outside and leave her on her own, as if he knew that she was going to be okay.

This was the first indication that Buddy was no ordinary dog. I'd always thought he was special, of course, but he seemed to have a sixth sense when it came to noticing that people needed extra care. That incident with Gran was just one example of Buddy's empathy – there's more to come later on.

Buddy was always great with people, and he was just as in tune with other animals. Even my feisty Hackney, Matilda. She always loved Buddy and was really good with him, dropping her head so that he could nudge her and lick her nostrils. It was as if Matilda was saying, "Yes, you're okay, I'll allow you to be one of the family." Buddy would lay under her hay net, and the two of them were quite happy to just chill out together.

One summer, I took Buddy to the riding holiday in

Thetford. He happily trotted along behind us whenever I took Matilda out for a ride along the sandy tracks. If I ever took Matilda for a canter, I would stop every so often so that Buddy could catch up with us and wouldn't feel left out. We were the dynamic trio.

Life was lovely. My job was going well and it was great to be back at the stables, being able to spend lots of time with my animals. Everything was on an even keel. One day I had to go out to collect some horse feed and Buddy jumped in the seat next to me in the pick-up truck. We hadn't gone far down the road from the stables when we found two riders who were having difficulties. Their horses were really playing up, doubling back on themselves and refusing to go where the riders were trying to steer them. I jumped out of the truck to see if I could help, leaving Buddy in the passenger seat.

I thought I'd only be gone for a minute or two, but the horses had other ideas. No matter how hard the three of us tried to lead the two stubborn equines out of the way, they were having none of it. Then, all of a sudden, we heard a beep-beep-BEEP of a car horn. It really shook us up. Every country driver worth their salt knows that you shouldn't use your car horn when you're close to horses, as it can really scare them. We all spun round to see where the commotion was coming from.

You won't believe it, but it turned out that it was none other than Buddy. He'd jumped into the driver's seat and decided to hurry us along. Not only that, but he had a hilarious expression on his face, as if to say, "You're taking far too long here. Let's move along, shall we?" The three of us burst out laughing. As for the horses, they weren't scared, thankfully, but they seemed to get the message too and finally moved on in the right direction. Buddy had obviously clocked how I made the noise with the horn and remembered how to do it.

Driving lessons would be a step too far, but I started taking Buddy to socialisation classes. Although he was good at the stables, I wanted him to be mindful around other dogs and, as he was a bull breed, I didn't want people to ever feel nervous around him. He took to the classes very well. I knew he was getting more confident when the agility tunnel came out. The dogs would calmly wait their turn to run through it, but my little Buddy would be champing at the bit for his turn.

When I said "Go, Buddy!" he would bomb through so quickly that the tunnel would collapse in on him and he would get stuck in the middle. He would be running around like a maniac, getting himself twisted up like a string of sausages. It was hilarious to watch. Best of all, it didn't bother him one bit. Eventually, he would emerge smiling as if to say, "My favourite thing! Can we do it again?" Other members of the class soon realised that this was definitely one Staffy they didn't need to be nervous about.

Since the day I'd found him, I'd been taking Buddy to see Ian the vet for check-ups every couple of weeks. Ian would weigh Buddy and check how his skin was doing. We'd always known that we were going to be in it for the long haul, but it sometimes felt like we were taking one step forwards and two steps back. Sometimes his skin had improved, sometimes it was worse. Like the other dogs at the stables, Buddy would often traipse through the mud, and I wondered whether that may have been aggravating his skin even more.

I'd also started to notice that Buddy would occasionally chew his tail. I don't know whether it was sore skin that had started to become itchy or whether something else was irritating him. But sometimes he chewed so much that his tail would start bleeding. If he scratched it and then wagged his tail, it would send an arc of blood spraying around wherever he was. The first time I saw it, I was horrified. It looked like something out of an episode of *CSI*.

I managed to bandage up his tail as well as I could, but Buddy hated the feeling of the dressing and would pull it off or shake it free, no matter how professional I thought I'd been. I watched YouTube videos on how to dress his tail properly, but to no avail. When I finally accepted that my efforts had been in vain, I bandaged his tail up one more time and wound black plastic gaffer tape around the outside to keep it all sealed (yes, it did look ridiculous, if you're wondering), and then off back to Ian's we went.

The vet said that the best thing to do would be to amputate Buddy's tail, but I couldn't bear that idea. Surely there was something less drastic? Hadn't the poor boy been through enough already? Buddy's little tail was such a big part of his personality. Ian understood my reservations and suggested we try a course of strong steroids and antibiotics instead. This meant more medicines for my little Buddy. Blimey, would there ever be a time when he was 100 per cent healthy?

As I say, one step forwards, two steps back. We started to see an improvement to the wound on his tail fairly quickly, but the strong medication seemed to have side effects. It was making my little Buddy depressed and listless. He would mope around and didn't seem to want to play. He'd lost his spark.

I was concerned that the steroids could weaken his immune system, which could put him at risk of developing demodectic mange for a second time. I didn't want him to have to go through that agony again. Poor Buddy's skin had always suffered from flare-ups, and it would be five years until I found exactly the right treatment for him.

For months, I felt as though I was going round in circles with Buddy on and off the meds. Eventually, I decided, after quite a lot of convincing from the vet, that amputating his tail was the best option after all. I felt terrible about it. I felt as if I'd been making all these big decisions for Buddy, and so far none of them seemed to have helped. At times like this, I really wished he could talk and tell me what he was thinking. He would look up at me with his sad little eyes and I would feel so helpless.

"I'm sorry, Buddy Dog," I would tell him. "I promise you I'm trying to do my best."

The night before the operation, in February 2011, I couldn't sleep, getting it into my head that something was going to go wrong and Buddy wouldn't wake up after surgery. I'm such a worrier. I knew the vet was right and that tail amputation was the best way forward. But Buddy's my baby. And here I was making another big choice for him.

It turned out that there was nothing to worry about. I dropped Buddy off at the vet and it all went according to plan. Buddy was a bit woozy when he woke up, and more than a little miffed to discover that he was now sporting what appeared to be a bonnet. But he was much perkier after a few hours once the anaesthetic had worn off. Back home later that evening, he wolfed down his dinner and looked perfectly content as we sat together watching television. It's remarkable how quickly animals can bounce back from surgery.

Buddy hated having to wear the cone though. He would frantically shake his head from side to side, trying to get it off, but it was a good distraction from his stitched-up tail stump, which healed remarkably quickly. Buddy would never look the same again, but he still had a little stump to wag and it didn't seem to take him long to get used to it. Because he was off the horrible meds, his spirit soon returned and so did my happy little dog.

It had been another expensive episode in what was starting to be an epic record of medical notes. Eat your heart out, *Casualty*. What with all the meds from when I first found him and all the subsequent treatment for his skin, it was a good job that I had a full-time job and weekend work at the stables to keep me going. I'd signed Buddy up to an insurance plan as soon as I'd found him, but the pet insurance company refused to pay for any of the treatment on his tail as they claimed it was a behavioural issue. After a letter from the vet, they reconsidered the claim and paid the bill.

In the end, the cost of his treatment was a drop in the ocean compared with how much one of Buddy's next medical dramas would end up costing me. But there were to be plenty of happy times ahead before that particular episode began.

A new person
enters our lives

A seemingly ordinary Monday in July 2009 was the start of another new chapter in my life. As usual, I'd woken up at 6am, dropped Buddy off and caught the bus to work. The weather had been glorious and we were well into wedding season with the horse-and-carriage business. It was lovely to be wearing light summery work clothes rather than having to be suited and booted as an official groom.

That day at the job centre, we had a number of new recruits starting. It was my job to go through their induction. This was nothing too formal, just a matter of talking them through the various systems. The new intakes all seemed nice enough. I was single but I certainly wasn't scoping them out for potential new boyfriends or anything like that. Buddy was the only male in my life at that time, and I was happy for it to stay that way.

We were all around a similar age and got on well, so it was no big deal when a week or so later one of them, Jon Owst, suggested that we all go out for a drink after work. *Oh, that's a nice idea*, I thought, *but it'll mean I'll be back late for Buddy*. I did go though, and it proved to be one of the best decisions I ever made.

Jon was really nice and I enjoyed chatting to him. He was tall with dark hair and had lovely blue eyes. He also had a kind way about him and seemed eager to hear all about my twin passions: Buddy and horses. We quickly became friends, going out for lunch together and catching up for chats at work, that kind of thing. We were just work friends though, nothing more. I figured I already had enough on my plate.

Around six months later though, Jon asked me if I would like to go to the pub after work. *Hmm*, I thought. *This sounds more like a date than a drink.* So I managed to get myself into a bit of a panic. Jon and I had become good mates and I didn't want to spoil that, or to make things awkward at work. I was a bit reluctant to go, so I asked my friend Rianne to come along too, in case Jon turned out to be some kind of weirdo.

He wasn't though, obviously. I knew Jon from work, so

I don't know why I'd put that idea into my head. I suppose it was because boyfriends before had turned out to be idiots, so I doubted my ability to judge a genuine one. I soon realised that Jon wasn't a weirdo, and gave Rianne a signal that I didn't need her to chaperone me anymore after all.

Jon is really into reading. He brought me a copy of his favourite book, *Shadow of the Wind* by Carlos Ruiz Zafon. I would never have picked out this kind of book for myself, but I thought it was such a nice gesture so unlike anything my ex-boyfriends would have done for me. But then again, Jon was totally different to other guys I'd dated in the past.

It turned out to be a lovely evening and I really enjoyed getting to know more about Jon. Obviously, I told him all about the big love in my life. I showed him the photos I'd taken of Buddy on the day I found him and also the more recent pictures where he looked so much better. I could tell from Jon's reaction that he was a bit unsure about Buddy, as he'd never met a Staffy before. *Hmm*, I thought to myself, *this could potentially be tricky*. But I understood his concerns as I'd also initially been anxious about Staffies. I told Jon that Buddy was one in a million and that, once he met him, he would love him too.

As the evening progressed, I'd gone on and on about Buddy so much that Jon could be in no doubt that my dog was the top male in my life. It was a case of love me, love my dog. Needless to say, I didn't use those words as he would have run a mile. But, to my surprise, at the end of the evening, Jon asked me out for a second date. What would I like to do?

We arranged to go for a walk in Bradgate Park on the following weekend. Getting ready on the morning of the date, I told Buddy that he had to be a good boy and show Jon how lovely Staffies are and win him over. Buddy never growls at people, but he likes to look after me, and I wanted him to know that Jon was a good one. I knew he would be a happy dog when he saw where we were going, as Bradgate Park is his favourite place to go for a walk – in fact, a popular place for people to take their dogs.

The weather was on our side and it was a fantastic day. Jon is originally from Middlesbrough and was really surprised just how beautiful Bradgate Park is. It's close to Leicester, but once you get through the gates it feels like it's in the middle of the countryside, with its green open spaces, streams, woodlands and lots of wildlife, such as deer, ducks and swans. I hadn't exactly planned it that way, but you can't imagine a more romantic setting. By the end of the walk, I think Jon and I were thinking the same thing: this could be the start of something special. Buddy was as good as gold. Despite Jon's initial concerns about getting up close to a Staffy, he soon realised that Buddy was as big a softie as him. What a relief.

Jon felt like a breath of fresh air after some of the other blokes I'd dated. But I did wonder whether he would stick around once he knew how busy I was outside work. At that stage, I was working full-time and was also busy on most Saturdays or Sundays with the carriage weddings. Only someone very special would be prepared to take on all of those commitments. I think it's hard for anyone who isn't horse mad to really understand, so I didn't think that Jon would stick around.

Owning horses is a bit like having children. They take up a lot of time, energy and expense, so it takes a special understanding to make any other kind of relationship work. But Jon knew how much my animals meant to me. He never made me choose between him or the animals; he knew where he was on my list of priorities. Instead, he quickly became a new dad to Buddy and would take him for walks while I went riding, or he would sit and read while Buddy had a nap. It just worked, everything and everyone slotting into place easily, and it was fantastic.

It made me realise how self-centred my recent ex-boy-friend had been (the one I'd split up with just before I met Buddy). At the time, even his mum had said I was too good for him. But I'd been smitten and hadn't really noticed the bad stuff. Maybe having Buddy in my life made me discover the things that truly made me happy. My beloved Staffy had made me wake up and smell the coffee. Life was too short to be with someone who only cared about themselves.

Sally and Rob also really liked Jon from the word go, especially as he was always willing to get stuck in and help out at the stables. He would fill up the hay nets, go poo-picking in the fields and generally make himself useful. It wasn't long before he decided that if you can't beat them, you need to join them. Jon could see how much I loved riding and said he would have a go. I picked out a horse for him: definitely not Matilda, who would have put him off riding for good, most likely throwing him off and stamping on his chest just to make sure he would never try it again. Instead, I tried him on a really lovely kind horse called Q, and off we went on a hack into the countryside.

Jon really enjoyed the ride, although, like most people, he found the rhythm of trotting a little bit hard on the old derriere. But it didn't put him off and he came out on rides with me a few times after that. He even cantered on a lunge (where the horse goes around in a circle), which is actually much harder than going in a straight line. I was impressed.

Life was good and, with Jon happy helping out at

the stables, we were starting to spend quite a bit of time together. It only seemed fair that I should embrace some of his hobbies too. And it wasn't long before the right opportunity arose.

Buddy the mountaineer!

The summer after Jon and I got together, we visited the Lake District. Having grown up in Yorkshire, Jon loved hiking in the countryside and was keen to cross Striding Edge to Helvellyn, near Ullswater. Thinking nothing ventured, nothing gained, I told him I would be happy to join him.

At that point, of course, I had no idea what would be involved. It's a quite challenging seven-and-a-half-mile trek, reaching heights of nearly 1,000 metres. I have to confess that I was slightly anxious when I read up about it beforehand. One guide described the route as "Daunting to the inexperienced and should not be underestimated! With its high levels of exposure this exciting ridge is bound to get your adrenaline pumping". I'd considered taking Buddy up with us, but I thought it would be too much to ask of him, especially as we were having such a hot summer.

I was quite fit from working at the stables, so I didn't find the hike up to Helvellyn was a problem. The getting down was the tricky part though. My knees started to really ache and I was in absolute agony by the time we finished the hike. I could barely walk for several days afterwards. I'd known beforehand that there was something going on with my knees, so maybe climbing the rocky ridge to the summit of Helvellyn hadn't been the best way to begin my climbing "career". But I'd never shied away from a challenge before and I'd reckoned my fitness would carry me through.

I loved the hike – minus the painful bit – and I knew that Buddy would enjoy an adventure like that too, once he was 100 per cent fit. We just needed to find the right place. And what could be better than the highest mountain in Wales – Mount Snowdon.

We started preparing for the climb by going for longer walks to build up our fitness. I wanted to make sure that Buddy was up to the challenge and, by January 2011, he was fitter than Jon and I put together. We decided that April would be a good time to go to Snowdonia, and started making plans for the big day.

Jon's Aunty Sue lives in Rhyl and invited us to stay with her. This was terrific as she's only around 30 miles away from Mount Snowdon. I was still a bit nervous about my knees, but I was more prepared for the hike this time, and we'd planned a gentler route down from the summit.

We set off at 9.30am on the morning of Saturday 9 April. It was a beautiful day, with the sun shining and a lovely breeze to keep us cool. There was no sign of rain, so this provided the perfect conditions for Buddy's maiden hike. I'd done my homework though. I knew that a sunny day at the bottom of Snowdon could easily turn into ice-cold winds and heavy rain further up, so we'd packed waterproofs with our kit. Like Jon and me, Buddy had his own little rucksack. But don't worry, I didn't overload him with crampons and hiking gear. It was mainly to protect him from the elements. His skin was still very pink around his belly, so wearing a little rucksack meant that he'd be protected from the sun.

Sue dropped us off at Pen y Pass car park, which is where several of the recommended routes begin. Although each route ends up at the top of Snowdon, some are more difficult than others. Each route takes around six to eight hours to complete, depending on its level of difficulty, so not surprisingly they are all classed as "hard strenuous walks". Eek! I just needed my knees to hold up.

We decided to take one route up and another one down, to make the most of the experience. On the way up, we took the Miner's track, which would be a straightforward climb for all of us. Buddy was fighting fit, so we had no doubts that he would be fine. We reckoned he would have run the whole route given half a chance, but we were determined to take it steady.

Buddy happily trotted along beside us, looking up at us every so often as if to say, "This is nice. Is it time for frisbee yet?" We took in the breathtaking views, keeping all three of us well-hydrated along the way. When we reached the stunning Llyn Peris Lake at the end of the u-shaped valley, we stopped for lunch.

We'd given Buddy a good meal at the start of the day and would feed him again that night. We were mindful that he mustn't get bloat, which is when a dog's tummy fills with gas and twists in a way that cuts off the blood supply. Bloat is a medical emergency, and I'd heard horror stories about dogs getting bloat after being fed without enough rest after exercise. Also, big-chested bulky dogs are more prone to bloat. So for Buddy Dog, there was a light, healthy treat, while Jon and I tucked into our sandwiches.

Three and a half hours after setting off, we reached the top of Snowdon. And what a spectacular view it was

– absolutely stunning. The weather had stayed fine for the whole of our hike, so we were rewarded with a view that few people get to see – 18 lakes and 14 peaks over 914 metres. A contrast of rugged green and brown mountain terrain surrounding blue lakes that were sparkling in the sunlight like sapphires. In the distance, we could even see Ireland. Even after our three-and-a-half-hour hike, Buddy was still full of beans, and he was certainly a talking point. People came over to meet him and say hello. Lots of them took pictures of our wonder dog.

Climbing Snowdon with Buddy meant so much to me. I thought back to that very first day I found him dying in the wasteland. Even I couldn't believe that this was the same dog that had been left for dead. Buddy was so happy and healthy, and with his help I'd been able to re-evaluate what was really important in my life. Life was about sharing experiences like this. It felt great to have tackled the challenge head on, and to have shown that I was physically and mentally strong enough to do it. Looking out across the stunning countryside and breathing in the air, this was a moment I would never forget.

One more thing that made the day so special was that it was my mother's birthday. I hadn't planned for us to walk on that day, it was just serendipity. I was so happy when I twigged that it was the same day. It was nice to feel her in my heart again.

I was interrupted from my contemplation by a fellow walker, who approached me to ask in all seriousness, "Is he a Sherpa dog?" Well, I suppose Buddy did look the part in his smart backpack. He was still full of energy as we set off on the climb back down. We decided to go back on the opposite side of Snowdon, the train route, as it was a much gentler descent. My knees were feeling fine, but I didn't want to take any chances. Besides, we were in no rush. It was one of those days that you'd be happy to go on forever.

The lovely gentle track down is called the Llanberis Path. Around two hours later, we'd completed our challenge of climbing the 1,085 metre-high mountain.

As luck would have it, there was a very appealing tea room near the car park where Aunty Sue was picking us up. We'd earned a cream tea, and that scone with jam and cream was just about the best thing I'd ever tasted. Happy Buddy thought the cream was pretty delicious too.

Happy ever after

Life with my favourite two-legged and four-legged boys was good, and I felt settled and happy. Jon and Buddy did too. So it wasn't long before Jon and I started talking about the next stage of our lives together.

On 7 August 2011, Jon and I went to our friend Ant's wedding in Brighton. The ceremony was wonderful. I have to confess that while watching the bride and groom exchange their vows, I couldn't help wondering when it would be my turn to walk down the aisle. We hadn't been going out for that long, but Jon and I were so good together. I felt certain that he was "the one".

You know what friends can be like at weddings. Catching up with the other guests beforehand, people kept asking us if we'd be next, joking about whether they should save up to buy a hat and stuff like that. Then, during the ceremony, looking out of the corner of my eye, I kept catching Jon looking at me. *What's he up to?* I wondered. *Surely he's not about to propose?*

I knew he would never do something like that in the middle of someone else's wedding – he would never want to steal the limelight – but I could sense something was brewing. And I was right. Later that evening, when we returned to our hotel room after the party, he popped the question. He didn't go down on one knee or make any big romantic gesture. He simply asked, "Will you marry me?" Then he presented me with a beautiful platinum ring with three sparkly diamonds. Needless to say, I said yes straight away. I didn't need asking twice.

I'd always set my heart on a particular venue, Hothorpe Hall in Theddingworth, Leicestershire. You reach this grand manor house through a field of grazing sheep and there are wonderful views of the Hothorpe Hills if it's a clear day. I knew that this would be the perfect setting for our wedding, especially if we were able to have a carriage pulled by Sally and Rob's beautiful white horses, Joker and Jester. Also, Hothorpe Hall has the added benefit of having wonderful dog-friendly grounds, which of course was vital for Buddy, who would be our guest of honour. But I knew that it would take the two of us a while to save up enough money to pay for everything. So it was going to have to be a long engagement.

When you tell people that you're engaged, the next question is always, "When's the big day?" We took a while to think about it. Because Jon is terrible at remembering dates, he suggested 31 March 2013, as even he couldn't forget 31/3/13. Of course, at that stage, we didn't realise that would be Easter Sunday. This probably meant the wedding ended up being even more costly, but it was worth every penny.

I knew that paying for a wedding could be eye-wateringly expensive. When it came to my dress, I didn't want to get carried away and blow the budget in one go. I asked Aunty Pat and Michelle to come along with me as my entourage when I went to choose a dress. I found a local wedding dress factory outlet so I had loads to choose from.

Despite having seen countless styles during my time working with Sally and Rob's wedding carriage business, I didn't have a clue about which kind of thing to go for. I tried on various different dresses and eventually narrowed it down to two, before finally settling on a really pretty dress that was fitted and laced up the back. My sister Michelle and two friends from the stables were going to be my bridesmaids. I chose coral-coloured dresses for them.

I organised more or less everything myself, as I wanted to keep it quite simple and we needed to try to keep costs down. My sister's best friend Liz kindly offered to make my bouquet of silk roses and all of the table decorations. We both had a little cry when she said, "Think of it as a present from your mum."

Every bride wants their mother with them on their wedding day. But my lovely Aunty Pat more than made up for it, being so supportive about all of my choices. She even made Buddy a gorgeous garland of flowers in the coral wedding colours. She was such an amazing woman.

Dad gave me away. In my heart of hearts, if I'm really honest, I would have preferred my brother Steven to do it. But I knew that it would hurt Dad's feelings if I didn't ask him – and also, how happy it would make him if I did. He didn't stop smiling all day.

Steven made a speech and, as expected, it was great – and really funny. He said: "Now that Jon and Nicola are married, the Bank of Steve and Steve's Taxi Services are now officially closed!" He'd helped me so much over the years with his thoughtful kind gestures and, as I was to discover, he would continue to push the boat out for me in years to come.

Our wedding day really was perfect. Thankfully, the

weather was kind. It was clear and crisp, and although there was still snow on the ground, the sun shone throughout the day. Sally and Rob drove me there in the carriage with Joker and Jester, which was wonderful, and they later joined us at the ceremony. Rob sobbed the whole way through it. I was so touched.

And as for my little Buddy? Well, bless him, when he saw all of his favourite people in one place – Aunty Pat, Uncle Steven, Sally and Rob – he became a bit over-excited. He was very vocal and couldn't stop chatting away with everyone, running from person to person. It was hilarious, but we quickly realised that there was no way we could allow him to come into the wedding venue. I could just see table decorations and elderly relatives going flying. Fortunately, he was quite happy staying outside with Joker and Jester – and of course he starred in many of the wedding photos.

Buddy the show dog!

The first home that Jon and I bought together was a little two-up-two-down in a village not far from the stables. I remember us going to view it and wondering what Buddy would make of it. After having so much space to run around in at the stables, living in such a scaled-down home would be a big step change for him.

Ideally, I would have brought Buddy with us, but it's not really the done thing to bring a dog with you when you go house-hunting. Knowing the misconceptions that some people have about Staffies, I knew it was probably best if it was just Jon and me. The sale went through very smoothly, and Buddy really liked the garden. There was a lovely dog walk for him close by, with big open fields on both sides.

He loved walking down the farm tracks and playing frisbee with Jon.

I started to realise that Buddy was a dog of many talents. What started off as a game of fetch with a standard plastic dog toy ended up being seriously impressive fielding, with Buddy leaping into the air to catch whichever shape we threw at him. Unfortunately, his prodigious talent also meant that he would help himself to other dogs' toys, sticks and frisbees. If we had a pound for every time we've had to apologise for ball theft...

Much as we loved that first little house, we really had our hearts set on another area nearby. We managed to sell the house quickly, but it didn't prove quite so easy to find a home in the village we wanted to move into. So it was back to Sally and Rob's stables for us while we kept house-hunting. I've lost count of the number of times I've packed and unpacked living there.

This meant that all of our furniture and other belongings would have to go into storage, so out came the packing crates and the bubble wrap again. I found it all incredibly stressful. I really didn't enjoy having to pack up everything again as it didn't seem that long since we'd moved in. We'd been living in the house for such a short time that we hadn't even unpacked some of the boxes from the first time around. Jon had so many books, he could have opened his own shop.

We'd been married for six months by that point. Everything was great between us, but the house move was starting to get me down a bit. So I decided I needed a day off from packing duties. Earlier in the week, I'd noticed an advert for a charity dog show in aid of Leicester Animal Aid at a local equestrian centre. I'd never been to a dog show before and I wasn't really sure what to expect, but I was certainly intrigued.

Watching Crufts on television, I'd always assumed that dog shows were for the elite. I thought they would be like some of the very posh, rather snooty equestrian events I'd been to in the past.

"That's not for the likes of you, Nicola," I would tell myself. "And certainly not for the likes of a scruffy old mutt like Buddy."

But how wrong I was. Buddy was in his element from the moment we arrived when he saw all those friendly people milling around, not to mention all of those wonderful new four-legged friends to run around with, bottoms to sniff and toys to play with. He was in seventh heaven. And so was I. Not the bottom-sniffing bit, obviously, but you get my drift.

I would often meet people out on dog walks, and I had plenty of dog-loving friends, but this felt different. *These are my people,* I thought. *These are ordinary dog owners celebrating their pets, no matter their shape or size. Buddy and I belonged here.*

I couldn't believe how lovely and relaxed the atmosphere was. Everybody was so friendly. So many people came up to say hello, crouching down to rub Buddy's ears and eager to find out more about him. I'm quite a shy person normally, but Buddy is such a happy, friendly soul, and he seems to somehow draw people to him like a magnet. People loved hearing all about how the two of us got together.

I met a couple, Neta and Jo, and their lovely lurchers, Mac, Indy Blue and Gracie May. The six of us seemed to bond immediately. I showed them photographs on my phone from when I first found Buddy. Neta and Jo couldn't believe that my Buddy was the same dog as that poor neglected creature in the pictures, or how healthy and strong he'd become. When I told Neta I was writing this book, I asked her if she remembered the first time she met Buddy.

"Of course I do," she said. "I thought he was adorable. I fell in love with him straight away."

Neta remembered warning me that Indy Blue could be a bit wary with new dogs after being attacked by a Labrador when he was a pup. But it turned out that there was nothing to worry about. Buddy and Indy Blue were instant friends and never had a cross word.

"What's more," Neta told me, "we're sure Buddy knew Indy's struggles and we're convinced he picked up that Indy was, in fact, ill." Indy was later diagnosed with an auto immune disease that ultimately led to his life being tragically cut short.

Buddy also got on well with their puppy, Gracie May. She was so tiny and could almost fit in the palm of your hand. It was so funny to watch my great big Staffy playing so gently with this tiny, delicate pup. To this day, when people see Buddy chasing Gracie May in a field or on the sand, I'm sure some of them must think he's about to eat her. Yet nothing could be further from the truth.

Anyway, back to Buddy's first dog show. It was the most gorgeous sunny day, and we went for a walk around the site together. Buddy was particularly taken by the barbecue and the stalls selling dog toys. Meanwhile, I had a look at the list of events that the dogs could take part in. There were so many to choose from, everything from Waggiest Tail (no good for Buddy, sadly) to Best Sausage Catcher (much more Buddy's sort of thing). It only cost £1.50 to sign up your dog for each event, so I decided to chance my arm and entered Buddy into the Best Rescue Dog category.

I loved the fact that the show was about ordinary dogs, rather than pedigree breeds. This was a wonderful opportunity for me to put all the stresses of the house move behind me for a bit and just enjoy watching Buddy having the time of his life. I could tell by the way he would prick up his ears before bounding off with a new friend that this would definitely be something we'd be doing again. I would insist that Jon came along next time as well. I knew he would love it too.

When the time came for the Best Rescue Dog category, Buddy and I lined up with around 20 other rescue dogs and their owners. I really didn't expect anything – after all, there were some seasoned professionals in the line-up. Standing there, as the judges made their way down the line that September day, the sun shining down on us, I looked around and smiled. No matter what happened, I was just so grateful that my Buddy was now well enough to even take part in an event like this.

The judges asked each of the owners questions about their dogs, and wrote down some notes on their clipboards. I was encouraged by the admiring reactions from the other contestants when it came to my turn, but I didn't really know how well Buddy had done. There were all shapes and sizes of dogs being shown, and I would have loved to have been one of the judges, finding out everyone's story. Naturally, we weren't being judged on which dog had the most dramatic story, but how they were thriving now and how good their temperament was. And my little Buddy was a star that day, smiling his best smile.

The next thing I knew, his name was being called. To my utter amazement, my Buddy Dog had been named Best Rescue Dog. I was chuffed to bits, never having predicted that Buddy would be taking home a trophy at the end of his first show. He'd won some dog biscuits too, which I think he was probably more excited about.

After this, the most amazing thing happened: Buddy was awarded Best in Show – at our first-ever competition. So from going with absolutely no expectations that morning, we went home that night with two trophies. Jon was thrilled to bits too. It soon put the boring bits of moving house into perspective. Life should be about the happy times.

I'd always known that my Buddy was a special dog, but to see the experts agreeing was fantastic. We'd been bitten by the dog show bug and were determined that there would be another one soon.

More buddies
for Buddy

After Buddy's beginner's luck at his first show, I was desperate to go to another one. Our next show was on another blisteringly hot day in late summer 2013. This time, Jon came along too. At this show, there were all sorts of different teams of mushing dogs, that would pull a kind of giant tricycle behind them and race. Most of the teams were full of huskies, but there was one team that caught my eye made up of lots of different rescue dogs.

Aside from the racing dogs, there was a small fun dog show. I was particularly struck by a lurcher called Scout who was wearing a collar and lead with the words "I am blind" written on it. After the race, Jon, Buddy and I went up to meet his owners, who were sitting nearby with their two other dogs. Their names were Tracy and Paul and as well as Scout, they had a pair of beautiful whippets with them called Izzy and Misty.

I asked if I could stroke Scout and said that I was keen to hear his story. Tracy told me that, like Buddy, he'd had a terrible start in life. He'd been rescued from death row after he'd been rounded up as a stray puppy in County Durham. Scout had been transported to the Midlands where they later adopted him, with 12 other waifs and strays from different adoption centres. Initially, he was thought to be deaf as well as blind and he had mange and kennel cough. At one stage, they thought euthanasia might be the kindest option for him, but he was saved again and given a new start, thanks to the East Midlands Dog Rescue.

Tracy and Paul were also keen to hear all about Buddy; they could see from his scarred face that he'd been in the wars. I showed them the pictures from the day I first found him and told them the story of how we'd nursed him back to health. Like so many people I show those pictures to, Tracy and Paul couldn't believe that my Buddy, sitting there smiling from ear to ear, was the same dog.

"The images in that album brought tears to my eyes," Tracy told me recently, "but to see the sheer joy and courageous spirit that shone from Buddy that day made me realise what a special boy he is. They say that some dogs are saved for a reason. Buddy always knew what that reason was, to share a lot of Staffy love far and wide."

Shortly after that event, Jon and I went to Greyhound Gap, another fun dog show at Walsall Arboretum. It included a Doggie Lucky Dip, Sausage Bobbing, Fastest Recall and other competitions to raise funds for Greyhound Gap, whose motto is *Helping Hounds into Homes*. It was wonderful to see the dogs in action, again having the time of their lives. Neta and Jo, the couple we met at Buddy's first dog show, were there with their lurchers, Indy Blue and Gracie May, and Buddy happily trotted along to say hello.

To our surprise, Neta and Jo were with Tracy and Paul, the couple from our second dog show. Talk about a small world. They introduced us to their friend Eluned, who was there with her greyhound, Ted, and another couple, Fay and Darrin, who had two greyhounds, Floyd and Hero.

As the dogs quickly got to know each other, so did we, swapping stories about our dogs and looking at each others' pictures. Hearing each other's stories, I was struck by how much we all had in common. From that day forwards, Jon and I had a new set of lifelong friends, all because of our four-legged companions.

Knowing how much Buddy adored my Aunty Pat and Gran at the stables, I wasn't at all surprised when he took a shine to Fay's mum Betty, who was also there that day with her crossbreed Cindy. Buddy really has a thing for an older lady, and they were firm friends from the moment they met. He would give her his biggest flirtatious smile and cuddle up close. Luckily, Cindy wasn't the jealous type.

We didn't just visit dog shows to come home with a trophy or rosette. The best thing about them is seeing dogs in their element, having fun, so we went along whenever we could. Over the following weeks, Jon and I regularly saw our new circle of friends on the dog show circuit. We'd get together with Neta, Jo and the gang, and plan which shows we were going to visit. We would make a day of it by sharing a big picnic and bringing along toys and treats for the dogs. It was great fun.

During that first summer, we went to a dog show more or less every week. It wasn't long before the shelf was filling up with Buddy's trophies and rosettes. He won in all sorts of categories – Best Rescue, Best Short Coat, Perfectly Imperfect, Best Under-18 and Golden Oldie, among others. Our friends' dogs, meanwhile, were always taking home prizes for categories such as Prettiest Bitch, Loveliest Lady, Best Long Coat and Waggiest Tail. Oh well, Buddy, you can't win them all.

One of my favourite prize categories was Best Mismatched Pair, won when Neta and I teamed up Buddy with Gracie May, her lurcher/Italian greyhound/

Bedlington terrier-cross. Gracie only weighs around 9kg, while Buddy is now a chunky 17kg, so they are chalk and cheese, but the two of them are best friends. The way they behave around each other is so sweet that the judges could see they were natural winners, and Gracie and Buddy won first prize. Incidentally, Buddy is now five times heavier than when I first found him in 2009.

Over the years, Buddy has sported lots of fetching outfits, including bunny ears at Easter, an elf costume at Christmas, a Count Dracula cloak for Halloween and a rather fetching tutu and pink headband at a dog show. Some people don't like the idea of dogs being dressed up, in case the dogs are unnerved by parts of the costume that flap around or distract them. But believe me, if Buddy doesn't want to wear something, he'll let me know about it and will soon find a way of shaking or pulling it off.

I've seen some great costumes over the years, everything from cowboys and Indians to Where's Wally and Raggedy Ann (that was Neta and Gracie May). One time I won Best Six Legs with Gracie May: I wore some brown suede boots and a pink cap to match hers. Another time, the whole gang of us – and our dogs, of course – dressed up as a football team and won. It's daft, but brilliant. We love it.

Buddy's all-time favourite event has to be Sausage Catcher. This is hilarious to watch. All of the dogs stand in a line, spaced apart so they're not distracted by their neighbour. The judges then line up and start to throw small pieces of sausage towards them. They start off close to the dogs, so they can get used to the idea, then walk backwards a bit. The dogs have to stay put until the piece of sausage is thrown towards them and then they have to catch it before it lands on the ground. Whoever misses is out of the competition.

Buddy has now become a real expert in this particular "discipline". Problem is, he's a SERIOUS sausage fan. Whoever has the misfortune of being his sausage thrower will find themselves being stalked by Buddy for the rest of the day. I am hereby apologising for all of his past – and future – sausage-stalking behaviour.

This being Britain, the weather can be a bit hit and miss. It's fair to say that dog shows are a lot more fun when it's sunny rather than tipping it down with rain. Buddy can't be doing with bad weather – he's just not interested. He'll put on the brakes when he doesn't want to go out, even if it's just a quick walk around the block. His front legs go forwards and he'll dip his head to try to slip his collar.

Unfortunately, not every dog show we've attended holds happy memories. In September 2015, we went to Pup Aid in Primrose Hill in north London. Pup Aid was set up by the television vet Marc Abraham in 2009 and supports a campaign against puppy farming known as Lucy's Law. It aims to ban third-party dealers, and to make all breeders accountable and transparent. If anyone is looking to buy a dog, they should be able to know that it's from a responsible breeder or shelter.

The campaign was sparked by the story of a Cavalier King Charles Spaniel called Lucy, who was rescued from a Welsh puppy farm in 2013. She'd been mistreated for so many years and kept in such appalling conditions that her hips had fused together. She had a curved spine, bald patches and epilepsy. This plucky little dog battled on for three years after she was adopted.

In May 2019, Environment Secretary Michael Gove put Lucy's Law before Parliament, and declared that the sale of kittens and puppies from third parties would be banned from April 2020. He said, "This is about giving our animals the best possible start in life and making sure that no other animal suffers the same fate as Lucy. It will put an end to the early separation of puppies and kittens from their mothers, as well as the terrible conditions in which some of these animals are bred."

Pup Aid is now a huge event, with loads of exhibitors, selling everything from dog food to luxury kennels. There are often quite a few celebrity dog fans there too, so it's great for star spotting. At that particular event, we met *Strictly Come Dancing* professional Pasha Kovalev and his partner, Rachel Riley from *Countdown*, as well as Penny Lancaster, Calum Best and Ricky Gervais.

As usual, we did a circuit of all the stands. Buddy had a lovely time catching up with friends and trying to coax me into buying him more chew toys. Jon is such a sucker for picking up merchandise at these events, and there's never any shortage of boutique doggy shops. I seem to remember we ended up with a fireman's costume that time. Buddy also had lots of selfies with celebrities who were bowled over by his lovely temperament.

I signed up Buddy for a couple of events and we went to watch the other shows and catch up with friends. We were having a lovely time, chatting away, when I looked down at Buddy and saw that he was covered in sticky brown gunk. Then, suddenly, he started choking. I tried to coax him to be sick so he could dislodge whatever had caught in his throat, but nothing I did seemed to help.

By now, I was causing quite a commotion. Luckily, Tracy is a veterinary nurse. She knew that it would be better for Buddy to swallow whatever it was that was choking him, rather than try to make him bring it up, so she gently rubbed Buddy's throat in order for his swallow reflex to kick in. The whole drama lasted only a couple of minutes, but time stood still for me while Tracy tended to Buddy. I really thought I was going to lose him.

Luckily, Marc Abraham was close by and spotted what was happening. He raced over to help and brought over a bowl of water saying, "If he can drink this, it means that he can breathe properly." I've never been so happy to see Buddy lapping up water.

Buddy had choked on a dog treat. The easiest way to describe it is that it looked a bit like a roll-on deodorant and contained a sweet liquid that dogs could release by licking the ball at its end. Trouble was, Buddy became a bit over-enthusiastic and dislodged the entire ball. He was lapping up the brown goo like there was no tomorrow, but the plastic ball had become stuck in his throat.

Thankfully, it wasn't long before Buddy was as right as rain. He started breathing normally again once Marc had managed to get him to have a drink. He was quite happy to finish licking off the rest of the brown goo too. Marc said there shouldn't be anything to worry about, but we should keep an eye on how Buddy does and that we'd no doubt see the ball again. In other words, once it had made its way through Buddy's digestive system. Phew.

That night, we checked to see if nature had done its thing and Buddy had "freed" the ball, but we couldn't see it. The next morning, the same thing. After a week of checking Buddy's "business end" and still no sign of the treat ball, we took him to see the vet and this time we saw Ian's lovely colleague Tim, who told us there wasn't much he could do. He couldn't feel the ball inside Buddy and, with it being made of plastic, it wasn't likely to show up on an x-ray. It didn't seem to be causing Buddy any discomfort, so Tim didn't reckon it was likely to do him any harm.

With time, we gradually forgot about the whole incident, and life carried on as normal. Then one day, virtually a year to the day that Buddy had swallowed the ball, it shot out of his mouth. We were at a friend's barbecue at the time and Buddy, cheeky thing, had sneaked off and eaten a corn on the cob. Dogs should never eat corn cobs: these are a choking hazard and can get lodged in their stomachs. In Buddy's case, however, it had the most surprising effect. The husk of corn dislodged the plastic ball and forced it up poor Buddy's throat at quite some speed.

Suffice to say, it was quite a shock, and we were straight in the car to the vet. We were hoping that it would just be a matter of monitoring Buddy's stools again and waiting for the cob to reappear. But unfortunately not. Tim informed us that on this occasion Buddy would require surgery to remove the corn husk. Luckily, we were able to claim on our pet insurance, but it was a valuable lesson for Buddy to learn.

After this, I did some research and discovered that there had been three other incidents of dogs choking on the same kind of "roll-on" treat. I complained to the manufacturers, who informed me that the dog treat was no longer on the market. In hindsight, I should have pushed the issue further. Buddy and those other dogs had a lucky escape.

Buddy's new home

We still had our hearts set on moving to our favourite village in rural Leicestershire. It's a gorgeous village, with pretty thatched cottages with picture-perfect rose gardens, impressive farmhouses and imposing manor houses sitting on plots of land bigger than a public park. I'd been spoilt at the stables, being surrounded by the countryside. Unfortunately though, we didn't have the five-star budget to go with our five-star dream.

We doubted we'd ever find anything remotely affordable when, miracle of miracles, a three-bedroom house came on the market. We immediately booked a viewing, but our hearts sank when we realised we could hear the busy nearby road from virtually every room. Also, the garden was the size of a postage stamp, which would have been no good for Buddy. With a heavy heart, we resigned ourselves to carrying on searching.

Incredibly, a couple of weeks later, another house came on the market. It was close to some lovely places to walk Buddy, and had the added bonus of being in the catchment area for a nice primary school and high school, a factor that had also become increasingly important to the two of us. Jon and I had "the feeling" the minute we stepped through the front door. We hardly dared to look at each other, as we were so excited. We didn't want to tempt fate.

As soon as we saw that it had a good-sized garden, it was a done deal. I wanted to run around screaming, "Yes, it's perfect! Can we move in right now, please." But we tried to remain professional and cool. We walked from room to room making noises to show we were interested, but made it clear that if we did make an offer it would be very much on our terms.

Ever since Jon and I got together, we'd known we wanted to have a family. We're surrounded by nieces and nephews, and we'd discussed having children early on. It's just one of those conversations that you have, isn't it? Neither of us wanted loads of kids – just one or two would be fine. There was no mad rush, so we decided we'd just let nature take its course.

For now, though, life was all about settling our number one family member, our wonderful Buddy Dog, into the new house. The moment we placed the sofa next to the bay window in the front room, Buddy bounced up and plonked himself on the windowsill, looking out onto the front garden and enjoying all the comings and goings as we moved the furniture around him. We put his favourite cushion on the window ledge, so that he could be extra comfortable.

"Oh yes," he seemed to say. "This will do me fine."

That windowsill is still his favourite spot to this day. When anyone comes over, they know to expect an enthusiastic greeting as he watches them approach the front door.

That first day when we moved in, I was conscious about how Buddy might come across to people who didn't know him yet. He likes to chat, but having a bark doesn't mean he has a bite. Buddy is a friendly, gentle soul, but he can be a little bit over-enthusiastic at times. If he starts barking at somebody walking up the garden path, it's because he's pleased to see them, not because he's trying to scare them away.

In fact, he doesn't have an aggressive bone in his body, and he would never hurt a fly. But I appreciate that Staffies aren't everybody's cup of tea. I was anxious not to worry any of our new neighbours, particularly any of them with young children. So I made a point of keeping him on the lead whenever we left the house, even if it was only to get into the car. I wanted them all to know that we were responsible dog owners.

Getting people to shed their preconceptions about Staffies too, wasn't a new thing. I was used to people being wary around Buddy, especially at the beginning, when we first brought him back to the stables and his coat was still in such a sorry state. I could see people wondering if I was the one who'd caused him to look like that. I used to get upset that people would make assumptions without getting to know the real reason why Buddy's face was so scarred.

I would always try to engage people and tell them the story of how I found Buddy. I know it's only human nature to be cautious, and I suppose other dog owners may have been worried that their dogs could catch mange from him, but the type Buddy had wasn't contagious. So I got into the habit of telling people what was wrong with him straight away to put their minds at rest.

I quickly became used to having to dispel people's misconceptions about Staffies too. I sometimes envy people walking their super-cute Cockapoos or Labrador puppies, knowing the amount of "oohs" and "aahs" they get from strangers. But I know there's nothing to fear about Buddy.

He's the friendliest, happiest dog you could ever meet. As soon as people get to know him, they quickly change their minds about Staffies.

Whenever I'm out walking with Buddy, I'm always careful to keep him at arm's length from any other dogs we meet until I've got to know their owners. I understand that some owners mistakenly believe that Staffies are dangerous, so I like to reassure them that neither they nor their dogs have anything to fear from Buddy. He's always as good as gold. He respects other dogs and behaves as if he's the bottom of the pack in any group of dogs. If another dog barks at him, Buddy won't bark back. He's confident enough, but he knows his place.

After I first found Buddy and his health slowly started to improve, I became aware that I would need to learn how to rein him in and stop him getting over-excited. Knowing how listless he'd been at the start, it was lovely to see him bounce around. But watching him tear around the furniture obstacles at Dad's house, I quickly realised I would need to find a way to channel his energy.

I sought advice from other dog owners and did some research online. There are lots of techniques you can try, but the one I found works best with Buddy is to get him to carry all of his own bits and bobs in his special doggy rucksack. When we moved to the new house, I bought him a new one in camouflage colours – it looked ridiculously cute – and off to the park we would go, with a little bottle of water in one side pocket and his poo bags and a toy in the other. Instantly, he was Buddy Dog the Sherpa again. Children especially loved him, and I encouraged them to come and say hello and give him a pat. It's amazing how quickly people can change their views about Staffies. I've always known Buddy's a complete softie, but it's lovely to see people patting him and genuinely being impressed by his temperament.

I knew that if we were ever to have children of our own, we certainly wouldn't have to worry about how Buddy would behave towards them. So once we'd settled in the house, spruced up the decorating and filled the shelves with Buddy's dog show trophies and rosettes, we started to think about our next adventure.

More dizzy heights for Buddy

After ticking off Mount Snowdon from his bucket list, Jon really wanted to do another big trek with Buddy Dog. A perfect opportunity finally presented itself in 2014. We'd planned a trip to the Lake District to celebrate our first wedding anniversary, and Jon set his heart on climbing Scafell Pike. We'd been up Wales's tallest mountain, after all, so he reckoned England's should be next.

This time, however, it would be just the two of them. After my first attempt at hiking, when we crossed Striding Edge to Helvellyn, I suffered from excruciating pain in my knees. Luckily, they held up fine when we climbed Mount Snowdon in 2011. But shortly afterwards, I had to have key-hole surgery on one of my knees, followed by the same operation on the other knee two years later. Neither procedure was a lot of fun and I had to wear leg braces for months afterwards – at one point, I wondered if I'd need to wear one underneath my wedding dress. Thankfully, everything worked out okay in the end.

The only reminder I have now is two small scars on my knees where I had the surgery. But after my knee drama, I reckoned climbing Scafell Pike may be pushing my luck a bit. I was more than happy to stay back at the gorgeous little cottage we were staying in and take things easy while Jon and Buddy bonded for the day.

Jon and Buddy did a fair amount of early-morning training in the weeks leading up to the climb. Jon was determined to make sure they were both as fit as possible for the challenge ahead. He would take Buddy out running with him in the mornings. They started off with half-hour jogs, gradually building up their stamina, and it wasn't long before they were out running for an hour or so.

By the time the big day arrived, in March 2014, neither of them could wait to get started. They set off at around eight o'clock in the morning after a big breakfast, again making sure Buddy had time to rest after eating so he was properly prepared for the exertions ahead. Buddy had his special little backpack containing his poo bags and sun block, and Jon had his human version, packed with

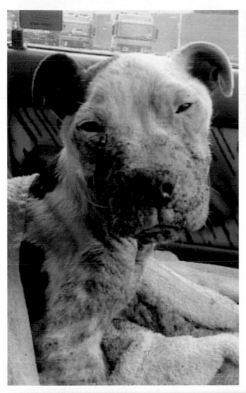

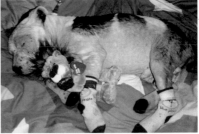

ABOVE Buddy resting, recovering, and cuddling his toy lion.

LEFT Buddy on the day I found him in April 2009. He was starving to death, riddled with mange and so weak his little legs couldn't support him. I carefully wrapped him in a towel and we were on our way home. My vet wasn't sure he would survive and said it was the worst case of neglect he had ever seen.

BELOW A few days after I found Buddy. I had carefully bathed him and applied cream to soothe his skin.

Buddy in his children's socks padded with cotton wool to help his poor paw pads. I think he was already starting to understand that he was loved and things were going to be okay if we were together.

Nicola Owst

AВUSE HELL BUDDY SHOWS AT CRUFTS

Miracle pooch on stage

A STAFFIE found near death on a rubbish dump represented his breed at Crufts at the weekend.

■ by PAUL DONNELLEY

Buddy was found locked in a crate on the outskirts of London by Nicola Owst.

At first she thought he was dead. But after a while he moved, so Nicola wrapped him in a towel and took him to a vet.

He weighed just 6lb – a normal Staffie weighs around 40lb.

The vet said it was the worst neglect he had his rescuer

live. Nicola, 34, of Kibworth, Leics, said: "I'm so proud of him. He's our little miracle.

"He was in a terrible way when I found him. He had mange and dermatitis, and his paws were raw from being in his own mess.

"He needed to have his tail amputated because of an infection."

Now 11, Buddy lives with Nicola, her husband Jonathan and their 20-month-old son Toby.

He took centre stage in the Discover Dogs section at Crufts in Birmingham, where visitors

ABOVE AND TOP In March 2016 Buddy was invited to represent Staffies at Discover Dogs at Crufts. He has been back twice more since then and in 2019 a national newspaper ran a huge story on Buddy and me that got more space than the Best in Show winner.

LEFT Fifteen months after I found Buddy, he was a happy and fit ball of energy. He still had skin problems but he was well on his way to perfect health. I was also the happiest I had been in a long while thanks in large part to my gorgeous Buddy Dog.

ABOVE We got our rescue Springer Spaniel Susie Sausage in June 2016. She and Buddy are great friends.

ABOVE Buddy loves being dressed up – if he doesn't want to wear something he will quickly tell me about it. I think he makes a very handsome Count Dracula.

LEFT My beautiful Hackney horse Matilda. Buddy loves his rides on the trap.

LEFT Buddy was the guest of honour at our wedding on 31st March 2013. My wonderful Aunty Pat made him a garland to match the bridesmaids' dresses.

BELOW Buddy winning a beautiful first place rosette and bag of goodies at one of the fun charity dog shows we love to attend.

ABOVE Buddy with Aunty Pat's mum Beat – she didn't remember me but loves Buddy.

ABOVE Buddy loves a game of frisbee and would play all day if he could.

LEFT Sherpa Dog Buddy! When Buddy wears his backpack we find people are much more likely to come and say hello. They soon realise that Staffies like Buddy are very friendly.

ABOVE Here we are at the top of Mount Snowdon, two years after I found Buddy. It was an incredible achievement to have reached the top and for Buddy not just to have survived but to have thrived. He's my absolute hero.

Nicola Owst

ABOVE When you have three little characters as cute as this at home, who needs to buy Christmas cards from a shop? This was the front of our cards for Christmas 2018. **BOTTOM LEFT** Buddy in the sand dunes at Sea Palling. **BOTTOM RIGHT** Buddy and friends on a Halloween walk in the grounds of Holkham Hall.

Jo Green

Buddy looking strong and relaxed soaking up the sun. He couldn't look happier.

Andy Biggar

sandwiches, snacks for Buddy and plenty of water for the two of them – and, of course, a map and compass. He reckoned it would take them around three hours to climb up, and then hopefully a little less to climb down.

"We should be back by three o'clock," he said confidently. "If we're not back by six, you can start panicking."

I wasn't worried, as I knew they were well prepared with all of their training and plenty of supplies. I was looking forward to spending several hours on my own and seeing them later on. Once my intrepid two explorers headed off, I got ready for a lovely relaxing bath and lots of television-watching.

There are a number of different routes up Scafell Pike. As I was later to discover, Jon took it upon himself to start his and Buddy's adventure with one of the steepest sections. It was really tough going, and at one point Jon wondered if he should turn around and return to the start. But he was already a good hour into the walk by that point, so he decided to press on. Buddy was having no trouble scaling any part of the climb – he was having the time of his life.

At least the weather was good. It was overcast but dry, warmish but not hot, so perfect climbing conditions. And Buddy, with his fine head for heights, evidently had no qualms about the route Jon had decided to take. He just kept skipping on up, pausing every now and then to wait for Jon to catch up with him. He did have double the amount of legs after all.

It's a steep walk up Scafell Pike to get to the top. You have to clamber over lots of boulders and hike over uneven terrain, so it can be extremely tiring and hard on the legs and knees. Jon isn't the kind of man to panic so, as arduous as he was finding the climb, he kept pushing on. He figured that if he kept going upwards, he had to reach the top eventually, which I suppose has a certain undeniable logic to it. I have to say I'm glad I wasn't there with them. I would have been seriously panicking by then.

Jon was mightily relieved when he finally reached the top of Scafell Pike after three and a half hours of tough climbing. Buddy was quickly attracting the attention of other climbers. Jon gave him lots of fuss and cuddles, and this put the other climbers' minds at rest that he was a responsible owner – and not someone who had just randomly taken a dog out to climb one of the country's highest mountains.

By giving Buddy lots of attention – and getting lots of love back from him – people could see he wasn't the kind of dog that was likely to turn on them. Jon and I always keep people's preconceptions about Staffordshire Bull Terriers in mind.

As you can imagine, there's a great sense of achievement

when you get to the top of Scafell Pike, almost 1,000 metres above sea level. There's a stone plateau on the summit of the peak – a great place to stand and look at the glorious landscape around you. Jon enjoyed drinking in the 360-degree views all the way from the Mourne Mountains in Northern Ireland to Snowdonia. He said there was an incredible sense of camaraderie with the other climbers and, having Buddy there, possibly the world's friendliest dog, made it even more fun. And what a place to have a picnic. He wanted to FaceTime me and show me the views, but there was no phone signal at the top, so he took lots of amazing photos instead.

After a short rest, Jon and Buddy set off on their way back. Having done the hard bit – and making it even harder for himself by taking an especially steep route – Jon was looking forward to an easier trek on the way down. So what did he go and do? He turned right instead of left. It was only when he met some walkers on their way up that he realised he was going the wrong way down. Faced with the decision of what to do next – whether to hike back up to the top of Scafell Pike and come down the right way, or to take his chances and press on – he decided on the latter course of action. Again, he reasoned, he was so far along the route that it would have added hours to the hike.

Mindful that time was pressing on and that he'd been

hoping to complete the challenge by around three o'clock, Jon kept going. He headed for a lake and started walking across the fields, accompanied by his trusty Sherpa, Buddy Dog, who was oblivious to the fact that they were taking a rather longer route home. As long as he had plenty of water and the occasional treat, he was fine.

By that stage, Jon told me, he started to get a bit anxious, as he knew how worried I'd be if he was late back. It was clear by then that his hopes of getting back by three o'clock were slim, but he still couldn't get a signal on his phone, so he couldn't call me to let me know. He was still crossing fields, and the finish line was very far away. Buddy, Jon reassured me later, was brilliant. He obediently made sure to keep to the perimeter of any field with grazing cows, as we'd trained him. As many dog owners will know, cows can charge if they're startled by dogs, and that was the last thing they needed.

More and more fields to cross, and more and more hours ticked by. Jon knew they weren't going to make the six o'clock deadline either, unless they got a move on. It was the last thing he felt like doing, but Jon started jogging across the fields, trying to make up a bit of time. If Buddy had shown any signs of distress or tiredness, Jon would have happily carried him, but it was all just a big adventure for the Staffy and he happily skipped along. Finally, they reached a road, and Jon worked out that it was only another half a mile or so to where he had parked the car. I wouldn't be surprised if he kissed it when they reached it.

Back at the cottage, I was clock-watching. I'd already started to fret (no surprise there, you're probably saying), but I was keeping to the deal of not calling the emergency services until after six o'clock. You can imagine how relieved I was when, only a few minutes before six, I saw Jon's car approach.

Jon practically fell through the door. What should have been a nine-and-a-half-mile walk taking between five and six hours ended up being a 23-mile walk taking 10 hours. Buddy, meanwhile, was still full of beans, wagging his stump like there's no tomorrow.

Jon and Buddy so deserved their baths that night, and they both slept very soundly. For my part, I was just so happy to have them both back in one piece. I think the experience put an end to Jon's climbing ambitions – for the rest of the year at least.

The C word

Life was ticking along nicely for a while until one day in early March 2015. I was cuddling Buddy, and noticed he had a swelling on his back left ankle. It was about the size of a large broad bean and it felt quite solid.

"What's this, Bud?" I asked him, as I looked more closely and gently felt it.

He didn't flinch when I touched the growth, so it obviously didn't seem to be troubling him and he wasn't limping or anything. He hadn't been licking the lump, so I didn't think it was causing him any pain either. But I thought I may as well get it checked out just to be on the safe side, and made an appointment at the vet.

We saw Tim the vet, who gave Buddy's leg a thorough

check-over. He didn't think the swelling looked sinister and wrote the words "Rest and Monitor" in his notes. And that's exactly what I did. I took Buddy back home and tried to get my energetic little dog to take it easy – which is easier said than done, as he's always so full of beans. Try telling a restless Staffy to put their feet up!

Two weeks later, the lump didn't seem to have shrunk at all. Buddy was due to have all of his annual boosters, so we went to see Tim again. He still wasn't unduly concerned but wondered if Buddy might have pulled a muscle or perhaps twisted his ankle. Whatever had happened, it didn't seem to be bothering Buddy in any way, so it was just a matter of monitoring it.

I wasn't convinced though. I had a niggling feeling that it was something more serious. After tying myself up in knots about it for another week, Jon insisted that I take Buddy back to the vet, if nothing more than to put my mind at rest and stop me fretting. He knows how much Buddy means to me. So off we went to Market Harborough again.

I was very apologetic about being so persistent, but Tim could see how worried I was. He said that I should make an appointment for Buddy to have an x-ray and to have some cells from the swollen area sent off to be tested. Of course, as soon as he uttered the words "cells" and "tested", my mind went into overdrive and I went into complete panic.

"Tim, are you saying there could be something seriously wrong here?"

Tim reassured me that he just wanted to be certain that there was nothing untoward. Even though I knew Tim was right – he's the expert, after all – back home afterwards I was straight on the phone to ask my brother and a couple of other Staffy owners I knew for their advice. One of them told me how his dog had had a couple of lumps and bumps removed over the years and everything had been fine. His dog's symptoms sounded very similar to Buddy's lump, and I wondered if it was the same thing, maybe some kind of bone growth.

Yet because Tim had mentioned testing some cells, I couldn't help worrying that Buddy had some kind of cancer. I tried not to dwell on the possibility, but I couldn't put it out of my mind. I typed the words "Staffordshire Bull Terrier common growths" into Google and the first thing that came up was an information box about mast cell tumours.

It read: *"Mast Cell Tumours (MCT) are one of the commonest forms of neoplasia in dogs... Although Staffordshire Bull Terriers are more likely than other breeds to develop these tumours, it has been suggested that these are more likely to be of the benign type than those that occur in other breeds (Dobson & Scase 2007)."*

As soon as I saw the word "tumour", I went cold. Even though it said that most of the tumours are benign, and therefore not life-threatening, I immediately thought the worst and convinced myself that Buddy was dying of cancer. I then started to read more and more about cancer in dogs. I know I'm my own worst enemy, but I'm not the first person to go online for information and ended up going down a wormhole where you find nothing but bad news – am I?

I couldn't bear it, not after everything we'd been through to get Buddy healthy after his terrible start in life. Buddy meant the world to me, and the idea of him having to go through any pain or discomfort broke my heart. As I sat in front of my laptop, tears streaming down my face, Jon hugged me and tried to put my mind at rest. He said again and again that there was no point in getting upset until we knew exactly what was going on. I know he meant well, but nothing helped. I was beside myself with worry.

"The chances are there's nothing wrong with him," he tried to reassure me.

The night before I took Buddy to the vet for his tests, he had to have his evening feed early as he had to be nil by mouth for several hours before he was given any anaesthetic. He was very confused, as I ate my breakfast and his own bowl remained empty. "Erm, hello? Mum? I think you may have forgotten something." I told him that he was going to see his friend Tim the vet and that he would have a special dinner when he came back, but you never really know how much dogs understand, do you?

Buddy was a bit subdued on the journey to the vet. He normally loves being in the car, sitting beside me in the passenger seat and smiling away as he watches the world pass him by. I sometimes wonder if this may be because he associates being in the car with being rescued, as that was his first journey with me. On this particular morning, however, he just curled up and ignored me. Maybe he was sulking because he hadn't been fed.

He didn't make any fuss when we arrived at the vet's surgery. He happily trotted off with Tim. I waited outside for a while, listening out to make sure Buddy wasn't in any distress. Then, hearing nothing, I very reluctantly set off for work. If I'd heard so much as a whimper I would have been in there like a shot.

I felt like a zombie that day as I tried to interview people at the job centre. Some of the clients I meet can be quite a challenge, but luckily not that day. I couldn't stop looking at the clock. All I wanted to do was be with Buddy. I'd rearranged my hours so that I could leave early and I was on tenterhooks waiting for the phone to ring. Finally, at around half-past two that afternoon, the vet's practice called me, saying that I could go and pick up Buddy. I was in the car faster than you can say "dog biscuit".

Back at the vets, Buddy was awake, if a little groggy. He'd been sedated for the x-ray and had some test cells removed from the lump on his foot using a technique involving a very fine needle. It was now just a matter of time waiting for the test results. Tim said he hoped we'd hear back from the lab within five days. Five days seemed like a lifetime to me at that point, but Buddy seemed oblivious to the stress. As soon as I settled him in the car for the journey home, he was fast asleep.

Buddy was back to his normal bouncy self the next morning, and Jon and I took him to one of our favourite walks. The idea that there may be something seriously wrong with him was hanging over our heads – well, certainly my head anyway – so it was hard to think of it as just another day. I couldn't help but think the worst – that it would turn out to be terminal and walks like this would be numbered.

I tried everything I could to take my mind off the situation. At home, I turned into some kind of super-charged housewife, sorting and cleaning everything that stayed still. Buddy looked at me as if I was nuts. I threw myself into every task at work, not allowing myself the time or the headspace to dwell on Buddy's situation. My lovely line manager gave me permission to leave work early whenever the test results came through. She's a dog lover too, so she completely understood what I was going through.

Friends would call every night to see if there was any update, and the "Buddy hotline" quickly became a support group for all of us. My friends were doing research of their own on dogs' unexpected lumps and bumps and kept reassuring me that if Buddy was suffering in any way, he would have let me know about it.

Five days after Buddy went in for the tests, I went into work knowing that today was the day when I would finally find out one way or the other about Buddy's lump. Even if it was going to be bad news, it was somehow better than not knowing at all. When the phone call came, the only word I heard Tim say was "tumour". I instantly started bombarding him with questions, but he was very patient with me.

"Come into the surgery when you can and I'll explain all the options," he said.

I was on my way immediately, desperately trying to breathe calmly and think straight so that I could get myself there without crashing the car. I tried to reassure myself that Buddy would be fine, but you can't help thinking the worst, can you?

Tim sat down with me and told me that Buddy had a mast cell tumour. He explained the difference between the three 'grades'. Grade one tumours are considered non-malignant and, while they can be large and difficult to remove, they're unlikely to spread. Grade two tumours are more risky, as their response to treatment can be unpredictable, and grade three tumours originate deep below the skin, are very aggressive and require extensive treatment. Obviously, the best possible outcome for us would be that it was grade one, but there would be no way of telling until the tumour had been removed and tested further.

Ordinarily, removing this kind of tumour is a fairly straightforward procedure for a veterinary surgeon. In Buddy's case though, the tumour was in an awkward place, and Tim was concerned that he wouldn't be able to remove all of it. Buddy would need to go to a specialist oncology practice. Tim recommended a centre near Birmingham. It was another long drive away, but I wouldn't have cared if he'd said we needed to go to the other side of the world, as long as we could get the very best treatment for Buddy.

I headed home to pick him up from my neighbour, who was dog-sitting that day. The second I saw him, I gave him the biggest cuddle ever and cried into his fur. I was an emotional wreck. I knew it would be hours before Jon would get back from work, so I called Neta and asked if I could go over to her house. It was nearly an hour's drive away in Warwickshire, but I needed a shoulder to cry on. I grabbed Buddy's favourite blanket and some of his toys, and we jumped in the car and headed onto the motorway.

I chatted to Buddy throughout the journey. I told him that in a week or so he was going to meet some new friends in Birmingham and that they would get rid of that lump so he'd be all better again. I like to think Buddy understands what I'm saying, but I suppose I was trying to give myself support as much as anything, trying to be positive about what was in store for him.

Neta and Jo were fantastic, as always. They completely get me and seemed to know just the right things to say about what I was going through. They understood why I was so upset and why I had gone from the word "tumour" to "goodbye Buddy" in the blink of an eye. That was the worst case scenario of course. Even if you're armed with all the facts, it's easy to allow yourself to think the worst. It takes much more effort to be optimistic.

I stayed with Neta and Jo for a few hours, then headed back home to Jon. When I saw him, I sobbed and sobbed again. All of the tension that had been building up over the five days of waiting for the result just poured out of me. Meanwhile, my lovely Buddy looked up at me imploringly.

He always gets very unsettled when I cry, and I felt bad for making him worry. But at that moment, all I could think about was losing him.

Jon, as usual, was really calm and practical. He adores Buddy too, but he's always much more pragmatic about medical situations. His default position was to be optimistic about Buddy. From what we read online, a grade one tumour was the most likely outcome, in which case Buddy would soon be as right as rain.

But no matter what Jon said, I couldn't help thinking the whole situation was my fault. Why had I left it so long to go to the vet in the first place? Why hadn't I pushed harder for Buddy to be tested from the moment I discovered the lump? I vowed that if I ever felt the slightest inkling that anything was wrong with Buddy in the future, I would go with my gut feeling and push for treatment straight away. No one knows your pet as well as you do because you're with them every day.

Buddy's Treatment begins

That night, feeling emotionally drained, I virtually passed out when I went to bed, though I only managed a few hours' sleep before the five o'clock fear crept in. My head started filling up with every possible scenario as I recalled the information I'd read online.

I started thinking about what would happen if, on further examination, it turned out that the cancer had spread into Buddy's leg. Over the next few days, thinking long and hard about it, I resolved that if this proved to be the case, I would ask the specialist to amputate the whole leg, not just cut away the swelling.

I was certain it was the right thing to do. Amputation sounds extreme, but I've seen dogs adapt remarkably well with only one back leg who can run around really well on three legs. If it meant that there was no possibility of Buddy's cancer spreading, then that's what I wanted the surgeon to do. Having beaten myself up about not being quick enough off the mark with the lump, I wanted to be fully in control of Buddy's treatment this time around.

I remembered how upset I'd been about having Buddy's tail removed, but I also knew how quickly he'd bounced back from that episode. Yes, leg amputation was a much more major operation than removing a tail. But, I told myself, it was a no-brainer if it was going to save his life.

When I let the specialist know what I'd decided, I think he was surprised by how unsentimental I was being about the situation, but I only wanted what was best for Buddy. The surgeon reassured me that he would do everything he could to remove all of the growth and keep Buddy's leg. Amputation would very much be a last option.

Prior to his surgery, Buddy had to take a short course of steroids to shrink the tumour. I was warned that the steroids would have side effects and, sure enough, as soon as Buddy started taking them, he developed a huge appetite. And boy, did he let us know about it. There was no keeping him quiet. Jon and I always say that's when Buddy truly discovered his bark. The operation couldn't come quickly enough for either of us, as Buddy was so noisy while he was on steroids and we just wanted the tumour gone. His constant hunger was particularly noticeable during the night before his surgery. The early dinner and the "nil by mouth" situation the night before is always stressful for the whole household, as Buddy gets so confused by any change in his routine. This time though, as well as confusion, Buddy was super-grumpy, as the hunger seemed to hit him harder than ever.

On the morning of the operation, Jon was feeling unwell, so Neta came with me to drop off Buddy at the surgery. Then once again we had the agonising wait for the call to say we could pick him up and bring him home. I went through every possible scenario with Neta. As I saw it, the best we could hope for was that the surgeon simply removed the lump and confirmed that the cancer hadn't spread at all. The worst-case scenario was that Buddy would need to have his leg amputated, but there was still a chance of the cancer being present and spreading. And then, of course, there were all of the scenarios between the two. Trust me, there wasn't an outcome I hadn't worried over.

Neta took me to the huge market in Nuneaton to try to distract me. Wandering around all the stalls, looking at everything from bird feed to tablecloths, I was in a daze, picking up things and putting them back down again, really not enjoying myself at all. But I was so grateful to Neta for being such a good friend. At two o'clock that afternoon, we received a call informing us that Buddy was out of surgery but would need to stay at the vets overnight to be monitored. The operation had gone well and the tumour had been removed. But the procedure had proven to be more complicated than the team had expected, as the tumour was wrapped around Buddy's ligaments and tendons.

Then came the words I'd been dreading. "We can't be a 100 per cent certain at this stage that we removed all of the tumour. Further treatment will be needed."

Further. Treatment. Will. Be. Needed.

I was desperate to hold my little Buddy, but the vet wouldn't allow me to visit him as he was still recovering from the surgery. They wanted him to keep as calm as possible and for him not to put any weight on his back leg. If I visited, Buddy may try to jump up to see me. I just had to wait – again.

Back home that night, I braced myself for another sleepless night. There was no way I was going to nod off, no matter how much I kidded myself. I ended up reading the same paragraph of my book at least a dozen times before I finally admitted it was never going to sink in. I don't think I managed to count more than three sheep before I became distracted. Time moves so slowly when you most need it to fly by.

Meanwhile, beside me, Jon was fast asleep. I couldn't believe it. I was tempted to wake him up and ask him how he could be so relaxed, but reasoned it probably wouldn't have been helpful to either of us if I did. If the situation had been reversed, I don't think I would have been best pleased.

The next morning I was out of bed at stupid o'clock. By eight o'clock, I was parked outside the vet's, waiting for the call to tell me I could come in and collect my precious Buddy. I was so happy to see my little friend again. He was still a little groggy after the anaesthetic, and looked a bit nonplussed to find himself wearing another cone of shame, but he appeared to be fine otherwise. He was sporting a very fetching dark green bandage on his back left leg, stretching from his ankle to halfway up his leg, and he seemed to be able to stand without any discomfort.

The vet was very positive about the operation, saying he was almost certain it was a grade one mast cell tumour and that he and his team had removed all of the cancerous growth. But in order to be completely safe, he recommended that Buddy have further radiotherapy and chemotherapy treatment.

Please, no, I thought. *Surely I'd made my feelings clear about removing Buddy's leg if there was any indication that there was some cancer left behind?* I couldn't bear the idea of him going through the stress of having yet more treatment.

The vet did his best to put my mind at rest. A short course of combined radiotherapy and chemotherapy would be a "belt and braces" approach to Buddy's cancer, he reassured me. That way, we could be 100 per cent certain that the cancer had cleared. It wouldn't take Buddy long to get back to normal afterwards, the vet promised – and what's more, he would have all four legs intact.

I had particular misgivings about the radiotherapy treatment he was proposing. It wasn't just that it would cause Buddy considerable pain and distress. It would also mean traveling to Cambridge for each session, which was a four-hour round trip, and was likely to require Buddy to be kept in a dog crate for a while, which he hated. He's always been claustrophobic, right from the time I first found him trapped in that cat carrier. Also, staying with a familiar vet is one thing, but I didn't think it would be good for Buddy's mental wellbeing if he didn't know the people who were treating him.

I had a long discussion with the vet about the pros and cons, and we agreed that we would try the chemotherapy route first. This could be carried out at Buddy's usual veterinary practise, so at least it would be in familiar surroundings with a veterinary team he'd got to know.

Buddy's treatment plan would involve eight doses of chemotherapy in total; once a week for four consecutive weeks, then every other week for the remaining four doses. All in all it was quite straightforward. This time I didn't need to drive myself crazy Googling information about chemotherapy. The vet was very upfront about all of the possible side effects. Loss of appetite, vomiting and diarrhoea were common. Allergic reactions were also possible, he added, although there shouldn't be fur loss. At least that was one less thing to worry about. Now that it was settled, the only question remaining was how we were possibly going to pay for it.

Buddy's plea
for help

I first arranged pet insurance for Buddy not long after I rescued him. Having previously insured Matilda for £5,000, I reasoned that £4,000-worth of cover would be ample for Buddy, given that he was a much smaller animal than a fully-grown carriage horse. And for a while, this level of cover was absolutely fine for him. I would pay off the excess and then each visit was assessed on a claim-by-claim basis.

Some claims were straightforward, like the time we needed to have the corn husk removed from Buddy's tummy.

When it came to cancer, however, the cost of the treatment started to rocket. Maths has never been my strong point, but I calculated the cost of the fine needle aspiration procedure to retrieve the test cells, the operation to remove the tumour and the specialist consultation. That's when I knew there was very little left in the pot to cover the cost of Buddy's chemotherapy, let alone the anti-sickness medicine the poor boy would need to make the process more manageable. It's at times like this when you wish there was a National Health Service for animals.

I was desperately worried. We hadn't been in the new house for very long and we didn't have any savings left. Jon and I were both working full-time, but we were hardly raking the money in. Friends and family kindly offered to lend us money to tide us over and pay for Buddy's treatment. But we didn't feel comfortable with the idea that someone else had to take responsibility for our pet's health.

Earlier in the year, Buddy took his first tentative step on the road to becoming a social media superstar after I created a Facebook page for him, called Buddy Dog – The Rescue Staffy.

I'd been thinking about it for a while because I used to post so many pictures of Buddy and his friends on my own Facebook page. I thought it would be fun if he had one of his own. And again, if it helped to spread the word that Staffies are actually lovely dogs and not the horrible fighters that they're reputed to be, then even better.

My first post featured the photo I took of Buddy the day I rescued him, alongside a more recent one of him looking fit and healthy. I wrote a short caption, briefly explaining Buddy's story, and circulated it to my Facebook friends, asking them to share it. I also shared the post to a Staffordshire Bull Terrier owners group and some canine rescue sites, not really knowing if there would be any interest out there.

Within minutes, I started getting "likes" and "loves", mainly from friends such as Jo, who commented, "Love can conquer all". But I realised we were also getting responses from complete strangers. One woman from Perth in Australia commented, "What amazing, caring people you are and what an absolutely beautiful little fella you have." Other messages wishing us luck came from a fellow Staffy from Maryland in California (it's amazing how good her typing was!) and someone from Dundee, who wrote, "Poor Buddy, I'm so glad he found you. Such a stunning boy." It was so heartwarming to know that other people cared about our Buddy Dog.

One of the first posts I made was a lovely inspirational quote I read about Staffies on an American site.

"We're not all fighters, most of us just want to give kisses. We just want to be loved and not judged. We aren't status symbols, we're dogs. We are what you make us. We come in many different shapes and sizes, but we all have one thing in common… We are Staffordshire Bull Terriers and we are softer than you think."

Then, on 28 April, the day Buddy was due to start taking his steroids, I posted, "Today's the day Buddy starts his cancer-shrinking medication. We're keeping everything crossed that the drugs do what they are supposed to do and shrink the tumour, which will then make his operation easier. We really hope the side effects will be non-existent. Come on, Mummy and Daddy's special boy. We can fight this!"

As the steroids seemed to be taking effect, I posted a series of three pictures of Buddy's swollen leg with the captions "Before medication", "Six days on medication" and "Ten days on medication", showing how much the tumour had already shrunk. I wasn't only telling Buddy's growing number of Facebook friends, I was reminding myself that things were moving in the right direction for him.

Gradually, the more pictures and posts I shared, the more Buddy's friends increased. When we learned that we would need to find extra money to pay for Buddy's chemotherapy, my friends Alison and Fay suggested that I also look at setting up a GoFundMe page to raise funds towards the treatment. *Why not?* I thought. *Nothing ventured, nothing gained. It's got to be worth a try.*

A few days later, on my birthday, my family treated me to dinner at a restaurant in the village. As it was a dog-friendly place, I'd brought Buddy along too. A couple was sitting in the same area as us, and I was conscious that they may not appreciate having their meal interrupted by Buddy.

"Be a good boy," I told him, "and stay close to us because these nice people are out having a special dinner too."

I needn't have worried though, as Buddy very quickly charmed them. The moment the couple spotted his little bandaged paw, they wanted to know what had happened to him. I told them about the operation and how he now needed chemotherapy, and the next thing I knew they had given me £10 towards his treatment. I was so touched that perfect strangers would do something like that. I've seen the couple in the village a few times since that night, and Buddy and I always say hello and thank them for what they did. If you're reading this, thank you again!

Theirs was the very first donation to our Buddy appeal. As word spread about our predicament, we started receiving contributions from people on Buddy's GoFundMe page and, amazingly, within just a few weeks, we had raised the £600 we needed to cover all the costs of Buddy's treatment.

I would log on to my computer and have tears in my eyes as I watched the total grow. I could understand people donating to big animal charities, but giving money to an appeal for just one dog, who in some cases they were never ever likely to meet, was extraordinarily generous. And for all the people who don't like Staffies, there are an awful lot of fans of them too.

Most of the money was donated anonymously, but I have a sneaky feeling that my brother Steven gave us a hefty chunk of money and that other dear friends such as Neta and Jo and Fay and Darrin put in some funds. We are eternally grateful to every single person who contributed. It meant the world to us. We felt very loved and supported.

I started posting daily updates on Buddy's progress and when his bandage was removed I shared a picture of his sore little paw and the 11 hefty blue stitches he needed after his op. I'd dreaded the bandage coming off, as I'd feared he may have to wear another "cone of shame". Thankfully, though, he was really good about not touching the stitches, and the cone wasn't required. Or at least not during the day. To be on the safe side, I made him wear an inflatable cone at night. It looked like an airline sleep pillow!

Having raised the money, we were now able to book Buddy's chemotherapy appointments. We still had a long way to go, but at least there was some light at the end of the tunnel. The night before we took Buddy in for his first round of chemotherapy, I was my usual anxious self. Knowing how severely chemotherapy can affect humans, I hated the idea of Buddy suffering even more than he had already. I'd managed to get myself worked up with worry and told Jon that I wanted to stop the treatment straight away if it made Buddy sick. Jon agreed; our poor little chum had been through enough.

The following morning, dropping off Buddy at the vet, I said goodbye to him with a heavy heart. I'd had yet another sleepless night and I was a bag of nerves, worrying about my Buddy. Waiting for the call to say he could come home, I posted an update on Buddy's Facebook page. It really lifted my spirits to read so many lovely, encouraging comments underneath his photo.

"Looking gorgeous as ever, kiss on its way."

"You're such a strong boy, sending love and hugs."

"We're thinking of you, wishing you a speedy recovery."

Thankfully, as I was soon to discover, I'd had nothing to worry about. When the time came for me to take him home, Buddy was there waiting for me, wagging his little stump and smiling away as if nothing had happened. I gave him a quick cuddle and, apart from smelling a bit of antiseptic, he seemed perfectly okay. Off he trotted towards the car and, jumping onto his favourite spot on the front seat, he had a little bark and told me he was ready to be secured into his safety belt and driven home.

It was as if he hadn't had any treatment at all. As I gave Buddy his anti-sickness tablet later on, you would never have known he'd had major chemo earlier that day. I'd had visions of me being up all night, mopping his fevered brow, but he was as right as rain. Apart from a little shaved area the size of a matchbox on his front paw where the chemo drip had been administered, you'd never know he'd had anything done to him. He slept fine that night – and as a result, so did I.

It was the same after his second and third chemotherapy sessions, and everyone was surprised by his resilience. It was a really hot summer and all he wanted to do when he came back home was to dive in and out of his paddling pool and go for a run with his friends. The chemotherapy meant he couldn't share his water bowl with his canine chums because of the toxins in his saliva, but sniffing and playing was fine. It was as if he was saying, "Cancer? What cancer?"

In October 2015, Buddy had his final round of chemotherapy. He'd had his white blood cell count checked before each treatment, and each time it had improved. The specialist couldn't say for definite that Buddy was completely home and dry, but with the swelling gone and his scar healing nicely, we were certainly on the home straight. It was such a relief that all my fears had come to nothing. It looked as though Buddy would once again be the incredible little personality we knew and loved.

Buddy goes to Crufts... and Scruffts!

For the next few months, Jon and I concentrated on getting settled into the new house and making sure Buddy was fully recovered. Our nerves had taken quite a battering with the whole tumour episode, so it was good to take stock of everything and get back to normal. Normal was a very comfortable place to be.

By the spring of 2016, Buddy was back in the pink and thoughts of his cancer drama were now firmly behind us. I was excitedly looking forward to Buddy making his first appearance at Crufts' Discover Dogs. Yes, you read that right: our Buddy Dog was going to be at Crufts.

We were first asked if we would be interested during the previous summer. While at a local charity dog show, we were approached by a lady and gentleman from the East Anglian Staffordshire Bull Terrier Club. The lady was one of the judges at the show, and she told me she'd been very impressed with Buddy's temperament, especially the way he behaved with the other dogs around him.

They wanted to know more about Buddy – and, as always, I was more than happy to oblige. I showed them photos from when I first found him and described how I'd nursed him back to health. As Staffy breeders themselves, they were horrified to hear how badly he'd been treated, and they were impressed by how well he was doing after his awful start in life.

They went on to explain to me how they exhibited their Staffies at Discover Dogs, the area at Crufts where members of the public can get to see different breeds of dogs at close quarters and chat to owners and breeders. To my utter joy, they asked if I would consider coming along with Buddy next year. Would I? Yes, please!

Crufts, of course, is where the crème de la crème of the world's pedigree dogs are displayed, but I was under no illusions. I knew my beloved Buddy Dog would never be a candidate for Best in Show. For a start, Buddy isn't Kennel Club registered as a pedigree Staffordshire Bull Terrier, so he wouldn't be eligible for the elite competitions at Crufts. Even if he was, he just isn't put together the way the Kennel Club judges require a Staffy to be. His ears sit too closely together and stick up on his head more than a typical Staffordshire Bull Terrier. And of course, there's the small matter of him having no tail and having been through the wars with his scarred face.

But I really couldn't have cared less. Being invited to represent Staffordshire Bull Terriers at the world's biggest dog show was a huge honour. Besides, Buddy had plenty of trophies and rosettes already. He won Best in Show at the very first local show he went to, and that was more than good enough for me.

I'd been to Crufts once before as a regular spectator. I'd loved going around the merchandise stands and watching the dog displays. If you've never been before, be warned: the Birmingham NEC, where the three-day event is held, is absolutely vast and you really need to do your homework before you visit. You can't possibly see everything in a single day.

Although Crufts has been going since 1891, Discover Dogs is a relatively new show. It was introduced in 1994 to help visitors find out more about all sorts of dog breeds, to talk to their owners and discover which kind of dog might fit in with their own lifestyles. At the Discover Dogs area, you can get up close to more than 200 different pedigree breeds – everything from the tiniest Chihuahua to the biggest Great Dane, and everything in between.

That first time I visited Crufts, I went with Neta and Jo and it was brilliant. I walked around the marketplace in a daze, trying to take it all in. Anything a dog owner could ever want is available for sale, be it gourmet dog food, a personalised mug, a nose-print necklace or, if you're feeling really extravagant, a £350 diamanté dog collar. I even saw a dog hydrotherapy pool for £6,000. Some people *really* love their dogs. You can also watch fantastic displays featuring police dogs, agility courses, Pets as Therapy, Medical Detection Dogs and so on. Needless to say, if you're a fan of dogs, you'll be in heaven there.

This second visit brought a whole new level of excitement though, as my little Buddy Dog was actually going to be part of the show. The reason we'd been invited to appear at Discover Dogs was to help educate visitors about any misconceptions they may have had about Staffordshire Bull Terriers. As I've said before, the idea that the breed is naturally aggressive is a complete myth. If you ever meet an aggressive Staffy, you should look at who's on the other end of the lead to find out why.

Knowing that some people have trouble appreciating just how adorable and friendly Staffies are, I had T-shirts and sweatshirts printed for Jon and me to wear. They had a silhouette of a Staffy on the front and the website address for Buddy's Facebook page and the words "Could you rescue a Staffy?" on the back.

I was really nervous walking up to the stand as a "newbie", but I was confident that Buddy would be his normal, well-behaved self. I know he's cheeky and can be a bit naughty at times, but he's a very obedient dog and is used to being around all kinds of other canines. The only thing I'd been a little concerned about was that Buddy might get a bit hot and restless being kept indoors all day, but we factored in lots of breaks so that we could make the most of the experience. I marked up on the map where the Staffordshire Bull Terrier stand was going to be, and I did my homework about the stalls I wanted to visit during our loo breaks.

Buddy had a special bath the night before, and I gave him a nice spray afterwards and brushed his teeth. He didn't need a pedicure; Buddy had already taken care of that. Generally speaking, it doesn't usually take Buddy long to get ready to meet his public, which is more than I can say for some of the other dogs I saw that first morning at Discover Dogs. I was amused to see some arrive encased from head to toe in special dog suits, to make sure they don't get wet or dirty on the way there − they looked like aliens! Some of the owners were quite eccentric too.

A lot of people-watching goes on at Crufts, as well as dog-watching.

On the first day of the event's three days, we made sure we were there nice and early. This meant we could soak up all of the atmosphere and allow Buddy to get used to the crowds before it became madly busy later in the day. The Staffordshire Bull Terrier stand had room for around six Staffies, and we were soon making friends with our fellow exhibitors and swapping stories.

From the moment the doors opened at 8.15am, visitors started to flood into the halls. It's unbelievable how packed it gets. The individual breed displays are the biggest attraction, but thousands of visitors come into the Discover Dogs section to find out about various breeds and visit their friends. It's a constant sea of people. Even so, Buddy will always manage to sniff out and recognise our friends, even when we're several feet away. One day, to test this out, we arranged for a friend to walk near us but not to interact with us, and Buddy went loopy and started shouting, "Why are you ignoring these friends of mine!" Obviously, it was in dog language, but we could understand what he meant.

By now, Buddy's Facebook page had more than 20,000 followers. It was so lovely that some of them came to Discover Dogs especially to meet Buddy, say hello and get their photograph taken with him. He was a real little celebrity, and he really seemed to enjoy himself.

It's a lot to ask a dog to sit and be patted for six hours, so each of the Staffy owners took it in turns to have some time out. Some went for a walk around the halls, others tried to encourage their dogs to have a snooze in their crates, covered with a blanket to make them a bit more relaxed. As Buddy refuses to go in a crate, I tried to take him off to a quiet corner for a little nap, but he let me know that there was something else he would rather be doing. There were always so many people who wanted to meet him and shake his paw, so he didn't really get much time off.

Typically, his favourite activity of all was visiting the pet food stands. He had quite the routine, presenting his most endearing smile to anyone who looked like they may have a treat for him. He became very good at showing off his puppy-dog eyes and putting up his paws on a counter as if to say, "That smells nice! Could I perhaps try a sample?"

After one or two circuits of the market place, Buddy developed a remarkable talent for locating the stands selling his favourite new treats, which is a clever skill to have in an exhibition centre the size of a small town. One time, he recognised one of the exhibitors from his favourite dog food stands when he was just taking some time out and buying a coffee. Buddy went straight up to say hello (maybe working on the assumption that he would have a pocket full of treats).

It was lovely to feel part of Crufts. Being there all day for three days was exhausting, but worth every minute. I really did feel that we'd helped to change a few people's minds about Staffies. And that, after all, had been our main objective for going.

Later in the year, a gang of our dog show friends entered their crossbreed hounds into Scruffts, the number one dog show for crossbreeds. Like Crufts, you need to qualify at one of the official regional heats to compete at the final, which runs alongside Crufts every March. If Crufts is the sensible grown-up of the dog show world, Scruffts is the lively little brother. It celebrates every crazy mix of dog, from Cavalier King Charles Spaniel-Bichon Frise crosses to Golden Retriever-Poodles. The event may not be as prestigious as Crufts, but it definitely has the loveliest categories, including Most Handsome Crossbreed, Child's Best Friend, Golden Oldie Crossbreed and Best Crossbreed Rescue.

In the summer following Buddy's first visit to Crufts, a gang of us went to a Scruffts qualifying heat. Neta, Jo and Fay signed up Izzy, Gracie and Bliss for the Prettiest Crossbreed Bitch category, while Betty entered Cindy in the Golden Oldie category. It's not unusual for us to enter our dogs in the same categories – there's never any rivalry between us, as we just go along to support each other. I think we'd stop going to dog shows if we were ever to get super-competitive. It's more about the friendship, the delicious picnics and the laughs.

I liked the idea of getting Buddy involved in Scruffts too, but first I had to know for certain whether he was a crossbreed or 100 per cent Staffy. When I first found Buddy, I recognised him as a "Staffy-type" dog and assumed he had bits of other bull terriers in his genetic make-up. Then, as his health improved and he started to fill out, he grew to look and behave more like a pure-bred Staffy. So I began to have second thoughts about him being "bits" of other breeds.

But with no paperwork or microchipping for us to confirm Buddy's ancestry, I still knew it was more likely that he was a crossbreed. Watching him play with his lurcher and greyhound friends, I was struck by how he seemed to share some of their natural athletic agility. I would look at other breeds, big softies like Jack Russells, for example, and wonder if maybe Buddy had a bit of them in him too.

It's never been a big deal, because Buddy's 100 per cent fantastic in my books. But I decided to get his DNA checked out, just for curiosity's sake. That way, I would finally know for certain. It was a very simple procedure.

I bought a home DNA testing kit online and, using the oversized cotton bud that was provided, I took a swab from inside Buddy's cheek – the poor thing must have thought, "Blimey, what's she doing now?" – and then posted it off to the laboratory for testing.

Around three weeks later, the results came through. It turns out that Buddy – drum roll, please – is 100 per cent Staffordshire Bull Terrier. It was neither good news nor bad news. When it came to entering Crufts and Scruffts, Buddy was in no man's land (or should that be no dog's land?), but it didn't matter. Sure, he could never compete in Crufts because of his wonky physical make-up, nor Scruffts because he wasn't a crossbreed, but it made no difference to me. Buddy Dog will always be a winner in my eyes.

More Testing Times

Jon and I had changed jobs a few times since we first met at the job centre back in 2010. We'd leave the house in the morning and he would go off in one direction and I would head off the other way. I was still working for the Department for Work and Pensions, but I'd had a couple of promotions and was now joint-managing a team with another colleague. To be honest, it wasn't a role I especially enjoyed. I'd always liked taking on new challenges, but while being in management sounds good on paper, I found this particular job unbelievably stressful – even more so after I discovered I was pregnant.

Jon and I were over the moon when we found out I was expecting. We'd always known we wanted to start a family, and this felt like the right time in our lives. It was May 2015. I'd only recently turned 31, and we'd been settled in the new house for almost a year. We couldn't have been happier. There was just one problem: I was suffering with the most horrendous – and relentless – morning sickness.

I used to drive to work with a sick bag on my knee and I would frequently find myself having to rush out of meetings to throw up (sorry if you're eating breakfast while you're reading this). My job also required me to meet with members of the public, and I would have to explain to complete strangers why I may suddenly make a dash for the door. Everybody was really nice about it, but it was all very embarrassing. I didn't feel very professional having to admit why I was so off-colour.

We didn't tell many friends or family that I was pregnant at first. It was still very early days and we didn't want to jinx anything. But there were other reasons too. With Dad's continuing health difficulties and poor Buddy's cancer scare, which was happening at the same time, we already had more than enough on our plates. Yet there was someone we didn't need to tell – he seemed to know.

They say animals have a sixth sense, and that's certainly the case where Buddy was concerned. He could definitely tell there was something wrong with me – and not just because I was spending so much time with my head over the loo. He would trot around the house following me everywhere, and would sit next to me with his head tilted, a little worried frown on his face. He wouldn't leave my side and, sitting beside me on the sofa at night, he would put his head on my lap and gaze up adoringly at me. It was as if he was asking what was troubling me. And, naturally, I told him everything – as I always had.

Pregnancy completely wiped me out. I felt exhausted from the moment I woke up until the moment I went to bed. I was normally so healthy and full of beans, but now I was a physical wreck. Jon was fantastic, cooking me light, nutritious meals that we thought I may be able to keep down, and taking over all the housework responsibilities. Then one morning, around eight weeks into the pregnancy, I woke up and instantly sensed something was wrong. For the first time in weeks, I didn't feel sick. I should have felt relieved, grateful not to be rushing to the toilet the moment the alarm had gone off, but something at the back of my mind troubled me.

Lying in bed, I turned to Jon. "Something's not right," I said. "I think the baby's gone."

I wasn't bleeding. *That's good news*, I thought, *and yet…* I couldn't put my finger on it, but I just didn't feel right. I know this sounds weird, but I felt human for the first time in weeks. I felt more energetic and, well, just more like my old self again. I even had my appetite back.

I knew enough about pregnancy to understand that morning sickness can be just a phase you go through when you're expecting and then it goes away after a while. I wondered if perhaps I was now through that stage and onto the lovely "blooming" bit. I asked Doctor Google and talked to Jon and colleagues at work who knew I was pregnant. Everyone said, "Stop worrying, it will be fine." Yet I still wasn't convinced, so I contacted my midwife.

She also tried her best to put my mind at rest.

"Have you been bleeding?" she asked me.

"No," I answered.

"Are you in any pain?"

"No," I answered again, realising I didn't really have anything to tell her.

"Well then, there's nothing to worry yourself about," she said.

That's all well and good, I thought, *but I'm worried. It's my body, after all.*

As much as I wanted to believe what everybody was telling me, my body was telling me that something wasn't quite right. Yes, I was beginning to feel like my old self physically, but I'd also noticed I was getting very teary. Mentally, I felt all over the place. Surely this wasn't normal?

Shouldn't I be feeling some kind of connection to this little baby growing inside me?

I made an appointment to see my GP. I needed to know what was happening, one way or another. I described how I was feeling, and he too told me that there were no medical signs to suggest there was anything amiss. "I think you've probably pulled a muscle in your stomach," was his diagnosis.

It's not that I wanted to hear I'd miscarried, of course, but this just seemed daft to me. Surely the reason I'd stopped feeling sick and was no longer utterly exhausted the whole time had to be connected to my pregnancy? It was so frustrating. As I walked out of his surgery, my parting words were, "I think we're going to have to pay for a private scan."

I felt angry and patronised. At my wits' end, I went online to do some more research. I started to read up on silent miscarriages, also called missed miscarriages, and I began to wonder if this was what had happened to me. It's not at all uncommon, I discovered, for women to experience miscarriages without any of the usual signs, such as pain or bleeding. Reading further on, I also learned that, as your hormone levels start to fall, the symptoms you associate with being pregnant – such as nausea, for example – may stop before you expect them to.

It all seemed to add up. However, the only way I could find out for certain was to have a scan, so I made an appointment at a private clinic in Lutterworth. If my suspicions turned out to be correct, I needed to know what I should do next. Would I, for example, have to go through some kind of labour to deliver the foetus if the worst had happened?

Stepping into the clinic, I felt a sense of dread. The waiting room was full of pregnant women, each of them looking so happy and healthy, one hand on their tummy, the other held by their husband. Jon was wonderful, as he always is, and he did everything he could to comfort me and keep me calm, but I just wanted to get out of there as quickly as possible.

I went into the consultation room, fully aware that this wasn't going to be that special moment you've always looked forward to, where you're hooked up to an ultrasound machine and look at a screen to see your baby happily swimming around. No, with me still being early into the pregnancy, this was to be an internal scan. It's a bit like having a smear, although you feel more exposed. The whole process only takes a few minutes.

Looking at the consultant afterwards, I could tell from the expression on her face that she was about to deliver bad news. She was very young, and I could see that she felt terrible having to say the words I knew were coming.

"I'm sorry," she said. "You have miscarried."

I can't pretend the news came as a shock to me or Jon, and it proved that my natural instincts were right – I knew my body better than anyone else. But I found the whole experience incredibly traumatic all the same; it was the full stop at the end of weeks of worrying. I understood that around 15 to 20 per cent of pregnancies end in miscarriage before three months, but this felt so incredibly unfair.

I was desperately upset and so angry that I'd had to find out this way, and that my midwife and GP hadn't taken me seriously. The nurse started apologising on their behalf, saying she was appalled that the onus had been on me to find out what was happening with the pregnancy. She was at pains to reassure me that the miscarriage hadn't been caused by anything I had or hadn't done. She explained I'd had a silent miscarriage, as I'd suspected. It wasn't possible to say for sure when the foetus had died. Because pregnancy hormones can continue to be high for some time after the baby has died, even if I'd taken a pregnancy test, it may still have come out as positive.

I still had lots of questions that needed answers, but I felt so shattered by the news. Jon and I just wanted to get home. We said our goodbyes, and the consultant gave me a letter about the scan results to pass on to my GP. I remember sitting in the front seat of the car in a complete daze as we set off home. I know now that grieving can sometimes take the form of anger, and at that moment I was furious.

I was angry with my midwife and GP for not realising that there was anything wrong, for not taking me seriously, for being so patronising. I'm an intelligent, grown woman. They could at least have the courtesy to treat me like one. I was also angry with myself, for not being able to carry Jon's baby, for not having a body that could provide the right conditions to let a foetus thrive.

On the journey home, I told Jon to stop off at the GP's practice first. I marched in and gave the receptionist the letter from the private clinic. I normally stop for a bit of a chat, but I was in no mood for niceties.

"I think the doctor needs to call me," I told them, before walking out the door and heading back to the car.

Back home with my two best boys, Jon and Buddy, I was able to sit down on the sofa and have a good old cry about everything. Jon reassured me there was no way the miscarriage had been my fault. He always knows the right thing to say.

"Whatever happens next," he said, "we'll get through it together, as a team."

As for my little buddy, Buddy, his gentle face and his

nudging cuddles were just what I needed. The next few weeks were going to be tough, but I knew Jon and my trusty Buddy would be by my side doing his best to make things better. Buddy and I had already been through so much together in his lifetime. Now, just like I'd helped to save him, he was going to help save me.

Later that day, my GP called me back. He was very apologetic about what I'd been through. It went some way to help me feel better, but nothing anybody could say would stop me dreading what I knew was coming next. Two days later, I had an appointment at the Leicester Royal Infirmary to have the pregnancy removed. As at the private clinic a couple of days earlier, I arrived to discover that the waiting area was right next to the maternity unit. *That's just what I need*, I thought to myself. It felt unnecessarily harsh.

Thankfully, I have no memory of the procedure itself. I was given a general anaesthetic, and I'm told it was a very straightforward and quick operation. That in itself feels strange. Having gone through weeks of thinking about a new life, removing it only took a matter of minutes.

It would be fair to say that I blanked out that day. Happily, Buddy was waiting for me when I arrived home, a big smile on his face. He looked after me, giving me special cuddles, which I know he sensed I needed. I don't think I even glanced at the leaflet about miscarriage and bereavement that I'd been given at the hospital. I was terribly upset and couldn't concentrate on anything. Jon and I had spent the last few weeks imagining how the first few years would be: thinking up baby names, talking about the kind of holidays we could go on together as a foursome, wondering about which of us the baby would most look like. So many hopes and dreams ended so suddenly.

Because I'd lost the baby so early, there was no way of telling whether it had been a boy or a girl. There wasn't a "baby" as such to hold, or to bury, so the whole thing felt very surreal. I'd had no bleeding or pain when I miscarried, so it almost felt like I'd just turned back the clock to before we started trying for the baby.

Over the course of the next few days, I was in touch with my closest family and friends to let them know what had happened. They all helped me start to feel better. Aunty Pat, Neta and Jo, everybody was so comforting and supportive.

After all we'd been through with Buddy and my miscarriage, Jon booked us a little holiday let in Swaffham in Norfolk, so we could all recharge. It was wonderful having time to re-group and stop stressing ourselves about the future. It was time for us to re-focus and start doing things that made us happy, like going for long dog walks on fabulous Holkham Beach.

Sometimes we're so fixated on thinking about tomorrow that we don't enjoy today. Jon, Buddy and I had each other and we'd been through incredibly difficult life experiences together. That was all that mattered.

A new arrival

Although we were all now happily settled into our lovely new home, Jon, Buddy and I regularly saw Sally and the gang back at the stables. I still kept my crazy, wonderful horse Matilda there, and I would always help out with the carriage weddings if my services were required. For Buddy, a trip to the stables, the place where he began his new life, was always a special treat, not least because it meant he could visit his best friend, Sally's mum Phyllis, and get lots of loving fuss.

Sadly, in March 2015, around a month before I became pregnant, Gran passed away. Buddy immediately felt her loss. He was used to her calling him in for cuddles and having lunch with her. The poor boy looked utterly confused as he padded around, searching all the places where he'd always found her in the past. It was so sad to see.

Sally, as kind as ever, said she was still happy for me to drop off Buddy at the stables during the week. But with Gran gone, I felt it was too much to ask. Sally needed time to take stock herself, to breathe. She didn't need an energetic fireball like Buddy under her feet every day.

Buddy loved our new home. Right from the day we moved in, the front window ledge remains his very favourite spot in the house. He will quite happily sit there for hours on end, watching the world go by, especially if it's a nice bright day and he can soak up the sun too. All the same, I've never liked leaving him alone for more than a couple of hours at a time. I used to leave the television on, so the house didn't feel too silent. We had a dog flap installed too, so he could charge around the garden whenever he felt like having a mad minute.

Seeing Buddy being such a happy, playful boy with other dogs, Jon and I had often talked about getting another dog to keep him company. Whenever we'd come home after being on holiday with our dog show friends and their hounds, I would notice how much Buddy missed them. He'd been around all these other dogs having the time of his life, and then suddenly he was back home with just two adult humans around. I always felt quite sorry for him and thought he must feel lonely. Maybe it was time for him to have some company.

Ever since I was a little girl, I'd always dreamt of having a spaniel. Jon and I had agreed that this was the breed we'd go for if we ever added another dog to our family. Shortly after my miscarriage, the subject came up again, and we decided that now was the right time to add another four-legged friend to our family. Well, I say we decided. Maybe it was more my idea and Jon was too scared to refuse.

Coincidentally, a local breeder got in touch with me. It turned out she had a spaniel bitch called Bracken who needed to be re-homed. The breeder was planning to send Bracken to a nearby dog rehoming centre, and I offered to take her there. It probably won't surprise you to read that I fell in love with Bracken the second I saw her. She was utterly adorable, the prettiest little dog I'd ever seen. Acting on impulse – yes, I know, it's a thing I tend to do where dogs are concerned – I suggested that Bracken could spend a night with me, Jon and Buddy. *You never know*, I thought, *I may just have found the fourth member of our little family*. Well, that was a mistake.

I took Bracken home and introduced her to Buddy. As always, he was a complete gentleman and happily stepped aside as she took pride of place on the sofa. We soon discovered, though, how much that little spaniel wanted to make her presence felt. The next thing I knew, she was barking her little head off at my Buddy Dog. She'd growl and lunge at him. Then, when Buddy refused to rise to the bait and start barking back at her, she proceeded to sink her teeth into his cheek – and wouldn't let go. Poor Buddy came trotting into the kitchen with Bracken hanging off the side of his face. He didn't look angry or in pain, just baffled by what was going on.

"Erm... Hello?" he would have said if he could talk to me. "So I've been trying to welcome our new guest and how does she thank me? By trying to bite my face off!"

He was so frightened he took refuge in the garden. I was so disappointed that there was no instant chemistry between the two dogs. It was just wishful thinking, I suppose, but I was still feeling raw after the emotional events of the last few months. I found myself sobbing that I couldn't give Bracken the lovely home she deserved. I felt like I was letting her down, but I knew there was no way Bracken and Buddy could live together. It was clear that Bracken would want to rule the roost, and that wouldn't have been fair on Buddy. So it was with a heavy heart that I took Bracken to the dog rescue centre to be looked after. It was another bitter blow, coming so soon after Buddy's tumour and my miscarriage. Was I destined not to have any more dogs, nor any children, in my life?

Happily, Bracken wasn't at the rescue centre for long. Within days of me dropping her off, she was adopted by a lovely family and re-homed. I wasn't at all surprised as she was such a gorgeous girl. Fortunately, we didn't have long to wait until another re-homing opportunity arose for us as well. Just a few days later, when I checked the rehoming centre's website, my eyes were immediately drawn to a new dog they'd taken in. She was a three-year-old Springer Spaniel called Susie – and she was absolutely gorgeous.

Just looking at Susie's photo on my laptop screen, I knew straight away that she was "the one". She looked so kind, a ball of silvery white fluff with a pretty mottled muzzle and a big splodge of black on her back. I'd always wanted a beautiful spaniel with huge round brown eyes and long floppy ears, and the perfect white line down the front of her face was the icing on the cake for me. She had mottled legs and little black feet, and her slightly wonky nose only made her more endearing.

I arranged with the manager of the rescue centre to meet Susie one evening after work. I remember the three of us – Jon, Buddy and I – nervously sitting in reception, all spruced up, keen to make a good impression. We were waiting with bated breath as Susie was brought up from the kennels to meet us. It felt like a job interview. Would we be good enough for her?

To my relief, Susie and Buddy hit it off straightaway. They each had a sniff, and there were no cross words between them. When we gave each of them a treat, we received a waggy tail from Susie and a waggy stump from Buddy. Who could ask for anything more?

Everything seemed to be going well, until the manager left us to get some paperwork and shut the reception door behind her. Little Susie was distraught. She started pining for the manager straight away, whimpering until she returned. I totally understood Susie's separation anxiety because of the way Buddy used to be with me. The manager had been the person who'd loved and cared for the spaniel since she'd been brought into the rescue centre. I began to wonder, though, if Susie may need more time getting used to socialising with strangers before she was ready to be re-homed.

I learned that Susie, like Buddy, had endured the most dreadful start in life. She'd grown up being kept outside in a filthy kennel, often left in her own waste. Her breeders forced her to give birth to a number of litters and also used her as a gun dog, but she became terrified of the sound of gunshot. She was kept in isolation for most of her life and was very timid.

When Susie first came to the rescue centre, she was in a terrible state. Both of her ears were infected and she was woefully underweight. Thankfully, when we met her, she was well on her way back to good health, but we were told that she would need additional medical treatment before she was ready to be re-homed.

I would have happily taken her home with us there and then. Our "interview" had gone very well, and the manager of the rescue centre told us that she was confident we could give Susie an excellent home. For the time being though, we would have to wait while Susie completed her treatment. We knew the rescue centre would give her the very best possible care. They would never contemplate rehoming a dog until it had been given a clean bill of health. They also always ensure that all puppies and adult dogs are spayed or neutered, wormed and inoculated before they leave.

After years of suffering abuse, it was exciting to know that Susie was going to be looked after properly for the first time in her life. *When she comes home to live with us*, I thought, *there will be even more affection for our beautiful new little girl.* So the day she moved in couldn't come soon enough for us. Buddy has always been friendly and sociable with other dogs. I felt confident that he would welcome having another canine in the house – as long as she didn't start clinging on to his face, obviously. If there was a time he was ever going to be jealous, it would have been when Jon and I first got together, and that never happened. Buddy and Susie would be new best buddies in no time, we thought.

On Monday 26 June 2016, we brought our lovely Susie home for the first time. It proved to be a difficult day for all of us, but especially her, the poor little thing. She hated the car journey from the rescue centre (she had a little pee in the car), and she was terribly frightened when we first carried her into the house. She'd previously been kept in kennels, and clearly wasn't used to being in a home environment. She lay down on the floor and made herself as flat as possible. It was almost as if she was trying to disappear. The feel of the carpet under her paws was a totally strange experience for her. And as for the television set and washing machine? Well, they were utterly terrifying to Susie, causing her a lot of distress.

I very quickly realised that adopting Susie wasn't going to be all plain sailing. She was clearly unsettled by the sensory overload. *Maybe this isn't the right environment for her,* I thought. *Had too much happened to her already in her short life that she was permanently damaged? Would she ever be able to settle with us, or in any home for that matter?* Her beautiful pleading eyes just made us want to love and care for her even more, but I had to be realistic that it would take her a while to get used to her new surroundings.

During her first few days living with us, Susie would cower and pee in fear whenever Jon put out his hand to stroke her. We quickly came to realise that she associated males with cruelty. She was much better with me, but her biggest confidante was Buddy. Thankfully, the two of them were best friends right from the start. She was the one who would growl jealously if she thought Buddy was getting too many cuddles, not the other way round. But with a little bit of gentle behavioural training, Susie soon learned all the house rules.

We quickly discovered that she's ball-mad. Not only will she bring you a ball wherever you are, she'll go flushing in the bushes whenever we're out and find a new one too. She has no interest in meeting up with other dogs or chasing them around. Instead, she just puts her nose to the floor and weaves around, hoping to sniff out a long-lost ball. She's always been quite a character.

It took a while for Susie to settle with us. And there were times when Jon and I questioned if we'd made the right decision as she could be a real handful. With everything else that had gone on, could we cope with more upheaval? But no matter how naughty she was, every time we looked at our cheeky Susie Sausage, we'd fall in love with her again.

On one occasion, for instance, I nipped out to the shop, leaving Buddy and Susie at home watching telly. They had access to the dog flap, and plenty of water and toys, so what could possibly go wrong? Well, I found out 20 minutes later, when I returned home to find Susie eating the carpet. She'd somehow managed to pull up an edge in the corner and was now happily munching her way through it. Yes, another trip to the vet was called for. Susie was fine, but the vet recommended putting her in a dog crate when we left the house in future. I felt terrible about doing it, but the vet explained that the spaniel would feel more secure being contained in a safe space with her favourite blanket and her toys.

Before I left the house, I'd got into the habit of always putting out rubber Kong toys containing food. Kong toys are very strong and durable, making them ideal for avid chewers such as Susie. They have other benefits too. Not only will the dogs be distracted by something bouncy to play with, but it also means they associate me leaving them with getting a treat. Now I do it every time, filling their Kong toys with soaked kibble that I freeze so they're like giant ice lollies. The dogs love them, especially Buddy, as he also gets a spoon of peanut butter in his (it's a bit too rich for Susie's tastes). I know, I'm a soppy so-and-so, but I can't help it. I just love my dogs so much and love giving them these treats.

Life goes on

With so much going on – Gran's death, Susie's arrival and still trying to hold down a full-time job at the Department for Work and Pensions – there wasn't time to dwell on my miscarriage. I was terribly upset about it, of course, but I knew having a miscarriage wasn't uncommon – it affects around one in four pregnancies. So I did my utmost not to obsess over it, and just carried on with everything else.

I've heard plenty of stories about women whose lives were ruined after a miscarriage, but I've always had the mindset that what was done, was done. It may, I suppose, be because of the way I was brought up. I was determined to draw a line under the experience and move forwards. I'm not trivialising what happened, and I completely understand the pain and suffering of miscarriage, but for me, my coping mechanism was to try to stay positive for the future. This meant giving myself a good talking to, taking advice from close friends and family members, and getting into the right state of mind to start thinking about trying again for a baby.

I've always been fit and healthy – looking after horses is very physical work – but I wanted to make doubly sure that my body could take a pregnancy. So I maxed out on healthy salads and vegetables, and Jon, Buddy, Susie and I went out for longer walks. I also decided to stop riding, as Matilda had such an unpredictable temperament. I couldn't risk being thrown off if I ever did get pregnant. I knew nobody else at the stables would want to take her off my hands, so I decided to put her out on loan.

I was worried that Matilda would prove a hard sell; her new owners would need to be very patient to win her over. Happily, however, we had quite a lot of interest in her, and finally found someone who was willing to take on my beautiful girl's somewhat challenging personality. I didn't want Matilda's new owners returning her within days, so I thought it was best that I was upfront about her personality from the start. I gave them reams and reams of notes about her, beginning with the following words, "The first two weeks of owning Matilda will be the worst two weeks of your life…" At least, I figured, everyone would have a fighting chance of making the new relationship work.

It turned out that I needn't have worried. Matilda and her new owners quickly clicked and, a year later, they bought her outright. Saying goodbye to Matilda was a real wrench, but there was no escaping the fact that she was a bit of a handful temperament-wise, so it was a relief to have that part of my life sorted. And as one part of my life ended, another began.

Within a couple of months of trying again for a baby, I discovered I was pregnant for a second time. Just as with the first time, I was hit by wave after wave of hideous morning sickness and overwhelming tiredness. Then, just as I was getting my head around the idea that this was obviously the way my body responded to pregnancy, all of a sudden it just stopped. No bleeding, no pain, no more sickness. When my appetite and energy came back, and I started to feel like my normal self again, I knew exactly what had happened. I'd miscarried again.

The first miscarriage had been devastating, but this time I was a little more prepared for the torrent of emotions that flooded through me. The sadness, frustration, anxiety, anger and hopelessness were all there again. This time, though, I felt more able to cope and was more practical and philosophical about it all. Also, as this miscarriage was even earlier than my first had been, I knew I wouldn't need to go into hospital to have the pregnancy removed. This time, I could let nature take its course.

A few months later, it happened a third time. If I found the second miscarriage easier to move on from than the first, I found this one utterly devastating. Having experienced the same kind of pregnancy and miscarriage three times in a row was more than just bad luck, I reasoned. I began to worry that I would never be able to carry a child to full-term. Surely there must be something wrong with me?

Buddy and Susie were there for me, as always, with supportive cuddles. In a way, I felt bad for wanting a human baby so much, as I already had two wonderful fur babies. But knowing that I could conceive but couldn't carry a child was deeply troubling. It was time to find out what was making me miscarry, so Jon and I made appointments to see the doctor.

We'd established a better relationship with our GP after that awful first time I was pregnant and miscarried, when no one seemed to believe that there was anything wrong. So we were reassured, if a little frustrated, when he told us there was nothing wrong with either of us. We were young and fit, with healthy lifestyles, and he couldn't see any reason why we wouldn't one day be able to have a child. It would just be a matter of waiting and hoping, he told us.

It was an anxious time again. I'm so glad we had Buddy and Susie to distract us from our constant worry that we may never have children. Having always assumed that we would, it was quite a step change to think that there may always just be two humans in our little family. At that stage, we didn't start to talk about fostering and adoption, or any of the other options. We hadn't set a specific date about how long we'd keep trying either. We carried on with life and kept hoping for the best.

The fourth time the gift of morning sickness was delivered, in the autumn of 2016, a tsunami of exhaustion hit me. *Oh no, here we go again*, I thought, already wondering if this pregnancy would also end in a silent miscarriage. Luckily, this time, because of my previous miscarriages, I was called in for earlier scans.

Jon was working on the day of the first scan, so I asked Aunty Pat to come along with me. She sat beside me as the consultant made all of the necessary checks. I hadn't had any signs of another silent miscarriage, but I can't deny that I was wondering if the consultant was going to tell me it had happened again. I couldn't bear the "not knowing". But this time, thank heavens, it was all smiles as the consultant confirmed that the pregnancy was as healthy as we hoped it could be.

Once I reached 12 weeks into the pregnancy, with everything proceeding as it should do, we knew it was safe for us to start sharing our news. I also had a copy of an ultrasound scan image of the baby to show people. I felt so happy and hopeful for the future. Given my past history, I knew I couldn't be totally sure that everything would be okay, but I felt like I could start to relax. With any luck, our family of four would be a family of five by the following summer.

More Crufts fun...
and drama for Susie

As a natural-born worrier, no matter how many relaxation techniques I tried, I was never able to completely enjoy my pregnancy. I would tie myself up in knots about it and ended up going to my pregnancy assessment unit three times, convinced each time that something had gone wrong again. Luckily, I had the fantastic distraction of another visit to Crufts to help take my mind off things. After Buddy's wonderful behaviour at the previous year's event, he was asked to represent Staffordshire Bull Terriers again at Crufts' Discover Dogs in March 2017.

This time around, Jon and I were much more prepared. We quickly decided that we would only be able to manage two days out of the four. Tired as I was with the pregnancy,

I loved the atmosphere so much that I knew it would do me good to go, and one day at Crufts wouldn't be long enough – or practical. Besides, Buddy loved it there too, and it was such a great opportunity for us to show Staffies at their best.

We had special leaflets printed with information about Buddy's life story and pictures of him looking happy to be with other breeds, children and other animals. I also included information about the breed, debunking some common misconceptions about Staffies. I handed out these leaflets whenever anyone came over to the Discover Dogs stand to help open up a conversation. When Buddy and I weren't working on the stand, we caught up with some of the friends we'd made at Crufts the year before. Once again, Buddy's winning personality was rewarded with lots of treats and free samples, including a very smart bow tie, collar and lead set.

We were stopped umpteen times by people who recognised Buddy Dog. I lost count of the number of selfies he had over those two days. It was just the tonic I needed. I would have loved it if there had been a rescue dog category I could have entered Buddy into, but that's not the way they do things at Crufts. And no matter what happens, Buddy is always my "best in show".

Whenever I've been stressed, my little Buddy can

always make me smile with his cheeky grin and his non-stop cuddles. As I grew bigger with my pregnancy – and no, the sickness never stopped, more's the pity – Buddy helped me to keep my feet on the ground whenever I began to fret. He's always been helpful around the house too, and especially enjoys washing up. If Buddy had his way, we'd no longer have a dishwasher. The moment he hears the dishwasher door opening, he bolts into the kitchen and gets as much of his body into the machine to lick every plate clean before Jon or I can pull him out again. As the top shelf is often full of dirty cups and glasses, he'll often emerge covered in whatever is dripping down from above. Susie Sausage is, of course, always happy to oblige too, with a few licks to clean him up.

It's been wonderful having Susie join our little family. But almost from the start she started having health difficulties, which I believe are related to her early neglect. Her first serious health scare happened in July 2016, around a month after we adopted her. She suddenly started to suffer from diarrhoea and became really listless. Her temperature had shot up; it should have been between 38.3 and 39.2 degrees Celsius, but it was well over that. I called Susie's veterinary surgery to let them know I was bringing her in immediately.

I whisked Susie off in the car, trying my best to keep

her cool on the way. The vet took one look at her and immediately put her on a drip, saying he would also take some blood samples. After a few hours on the drip, she seemed to have perked up dramatically, and I was told that I could take her home. Sadly, however, it wasn't to be. Just minutes after Susie was taken off the drip, she began to go rapidly downhill again. There was definitely something wrong. The vet said Susie would have to stay in the hospital for a few days while they tried to get to the bottom of the problem. They then took scans of her liver and pancreas. I hated leaving her caged up looking so sick and frail. Saying goodbye to those pleading puppy-dog eyes was heartbreaking.

Fortunately, I was allowed to visit her, and she really picked up when I took Buddy in to see her too. Susie's little face lit up when she saw him, and she wagged her tail almost in time with him wagging his stump. It was delightful to see them together. A few days later, once Susie had started eating and going to the toilet properly again, I was finally allowed to take her home. The vet said he believed she had pancreatitis and I was given medication for her.

All was fine for a little while, but then Susie developed stomach problems again. She started squatting in the garden but wasn't able to go to the toilet, and once again her temperature was very high. As this was a recurring

problem, the vet referred her to the same specialist veterinary centre that Buddy had been to for his tumour. It
meant a longer drive, but I wanted to make sure I had
the right diagnosis for her. Having had such a scare with
Buddy, I wanted to make the right decision quickly.

The "new" vet said that he didn't think Susie had
pancreatitis at all. Instead, he tested her for meningitis
and an immune system condition called polyarthritis. The
word "meningitis" filled me with horror, but I knew I was
in the right place for Susie to get the best treatment. The
vet later confirmed that Susie had an autoimmune disease
that could be controlled with medication. Unfortunately,
this means that our lovely Susie Sausage will be on steroids
for the rest of her life, but she only has to take them on
alternate days.

We had already started her on a low-fat diet, due to the
pancreatitis diagnosis, but it didn't work out well. After a
few weeks, she started to lose weight and I began to wonder
if there may be a problem with the food I was giving her.
Her dog food just didn't seem to have enough goodness
in it; at one point, she looked as if she was wasting away.
Knowing that a healthy diet is every bit as important for
our four-legged friends as it is for humans, I've always
taken a keen interest in dog nutrition – so much so, in fact,
that someone who overheard me talking about it at the

vet's once genuinely mistook me for a dog nutritionist.

I started doing some more research. I was on a mission to find some new low-fat diet food that would really help her. Thank goodness for Google: a few changes to her diet and, hey presto, we had waggy tails all round. Well, a tail and a stump, but you get my drift.

My poor little Susie has really had a hard time of it, and the steroids and low-fat diet mean she now has quite a sparse coat. But even though she has had a few health worries over the years, I know she's happy. Besides, her brother Buddy will always look after her. They really are great friends together. They may niggle occasionally – who doesn't? – but they are perfect mismatched siblings. I never had any doubt that they would be fantastic with the new baby too.

Hello, goodbye

As we approached my due date, I was doing everything I could to keep myself as calm and relaxed as possible. I was excited about becoming a mother for the first time, but Dad's deteriorating health was giving me real cause for concern. He'd started behaving very strangely. One day, for instance, he started attacking his settee with a knife, saying he thought someone was stuck in it. On another occasion, he worked himself up into a terrible panic thinking that he'd lost my sister Michelle and my niece Brogan. He was convinced that he'd taken them out for the day in his van and lost them along the way. As it turned out, he hadn't even been with them that day.

He also became quite forgetful. Visiting him one time,

he looked at my pregnancy bump and said, "You kept that quiet", even though he'd known about the baby since my 12-week scan. It was heartbreaking. His doctor told us this could have been as a result of a bladder infection, or possibly a form of dementia. After everything Dad had been through, it was another worrying addition to the list of health conditions he had to endure.

Dad had been in and out of hospital for a few years now, and as his cancer worsened, the stays became longer. At the start of June 2017, with no beds available in the local oncology ward, he was moved to an infectious diseases ward. With me being so far along in my pregnancy, I was told I couldn't visit him. My due date was during the first week of July, and I began to wonder if Dad would live long enough to meet his baby grandchild.

Despite the rocky relationship we had together when I was younger, we'd grown so much closer in the past few years and it was awful not being able to visit him. It didn't get any easier when he was subsequently transferred to different hospitals. During the course of all this toing and froing, he suffered a serious fall and fractured his neck. It was so upsetting for all the family to see him lying in his hospital bed wearing a neck brace. We were appalled that this had ever been allowed to happen.

Meanwhile, I was having dramas of my own. Around

three weeks before my due date, I became convinced that the baby had stopped moving. I'd had regular scans throughout the pregnancy and had been reassured time and time again that everything was on track for a healthy delivery. But the stress was getting too much for me, and I was desperately worried that I'd lost the baby.

With me being so far along with the pregnancy, it was agreed that it would be best if the baby was induced. So on 20 June, I was admitted to Leicester Royal Infirmary. The only person Jon and I told was Aunty Pat, who had offered to look after Buddy and Susie for us. The rest of the family already had enough to worry about with Dad.

After being given the treatment to induce contractions, nothing happened for two days. Then, suddenly, I started to get the most agonising stabbing pains in my left side and was violently sick. The midwife gave me another scan and assured me that all was well with my baby. I was moved to a quiet room, so that I could try to relax and maybe get some sleep.

Shortly afterwards, while taking a walk, miracle of miracles, my waters broke. For some reason, I thought I should mop it up, so there I was on my hands and knees when the nurse found me and told me off. Because of my history of miscarrying, I was classed as high risk. I also had joint hypermobility syndrome, which meant I wasn't able to have an epidural because of the health risks, so my bouncing eight-pound baby was delivered very quickly with just gas and air.

At 2.44 am on Friday 23 June 2017, Jon and I said hello to our baby son for the first time. We were left alone in the room so that I could hold our baby, skin to skin, and start to bond with him. No words can really describe what it's like to hold a human being that you've created in your arms. Yes, I'd carried him inside me for all those months, but feeling the weight of his little body against mine, and his heart beating against mine, was extraordinary. Jon and I looked at each other with tears in our eyes and couldn't take it all in. A beautiful living, breathing baby with perfect fingers and toes. Perfect in every way.

Later that morning, I texted a picture of my baby to Dad with the words "Hello Grandpa", wondering if the two of them would ever meet. My emotions were all over the place. I was so full of happiness and love for our new baby, but so sad about Dad.

The first few days of motherhood were all a bit of a blur, with me trying to learn how to be a mum. Like a lot of new mothers, I found it hard to feed the baby at first, but we soon got the hang of it. He didn't have a name to begin with. Jon and I had thought of lots of pretty names if the baby was a girl, but we were stuck for what to call a boy as all the good ones seemed to have been taken by family and friends. We liked old-fashioned names and eventually settled on Toby. It wasn't just that neither of us knew anyone else called Toby, but somehow the name really seemed to suit him.

Four days after Toby was born, we received alarming news about Dad. It turned out that he'd booked himself a taxi and, without telling a soul, left the hospital. He went home, had a shower and a shave, changed the battery in his electric wheelchair and took himself off for a haircut. After that, he went next door to visit Aunty Pat, who was looking after his new dog Poppy, and said goodbye to the pair of them. Happy that he'd done everything he'd set out to do, he then took himself back to the hospital. The following day, Dad went into a coma.

Taking Toby to meet his grandad for the first time was one of the strangest experiences of my life. I was saying goodbye to Dad only a matter of days after I'd said hello to the new generation of the family. Obviously, there was no way that Toby would ever remember the experience, but it was important for me to show Dad his new grandson. There was no flicker of recognition from him, but I would like to think he knew we were there.

Dad died the following morning, with Michelle at his bedside. I'd obviously experienced dying before – and was discovering that it felt different each time it happened, depending on your relationship with the person. No, he hadn't been a good dad when I was growing up, but when all's said and done, he was still my father, responsible for 50 per cent of my DNA.

I understood that Dad never set out to be cruel to me when I was a child. Although it took us a while, I was pleased that we'd eventually repaired our relationship, in no small part thanks to Buddy. The way Dad had helped to nurse him back to good health and looked after him when I was at work meant so much to me. Dad had never actually said sorry, but what he did for Buddy felt like an unspoken apology.

I'd grown to know Dad better over the years. They say that what doesn't kill you makes you stronger. I suppose my difficult childhood may have been part of the reason I'd grown up to be so strong and independent. One part of my life had ended, but a new one had begun.

Buddy and Susie meet Toby

Jon and I were conscious that having a new baby in the house could cause Buddy and Susie to become unsettled or jealous. So we were determined to try to make the whole process as stress-free as possible for everyone concerned. I was confident that they would be as good as gold with Toby – they'd always behaved impeccably around babies and young children in the past, after all. But they'd already been forced to adjust their normal routine during my prolonged hospital stay. I wanted to be sure that we were as prepared as we could be for when we first introduced Toby to them.

Each evening after visiting me and Toby in hospital, Jon would return home with the blanket that our baby had been wrapped in while we were holding and feeding him that day. The idea was that Buddy and Susie would then be able to have a good sniff of the blanket and start to get to know Toby's scent.

Jon remembers Buddy picking up on the various different smells on the blanket the very first time he brought it back from the hospital. Buddy started looking around for me in his quizzical way, as if to say, "I know she's here somewhere because I can smell her. And yes, I can smell you, too, Jon… But I'm picking up another human here. What's this all about then?" As Toby and I were in the maternity unit for a few days, Jon was able to do the blanket routine a few times. Each time he came back to the house, Buddy and Susie became more curious. The ploy seemed to be working a treat.

Toby and I came home on 26 June, three days after I gave birth. And what a welcome we received. I was concerned that Buddy and Susie may go a bit bonkers when they saw me getting out of the car and upset Toby with all their barking, but my beautiful little baby boy slept all the way through their first meeting. Meanwhile, I was given the most welcoming reception I've ever had. There was a lot of barking, running back and forth, and toys being presented before I'd even managed to get out of the car. There was so much tail and stump wagging, and their little nostrils were working overtime to take it all in. They were so intrigued by the little bundle I was holding. They didn't seem anxious in any way, just very excited to have me back home.

Flooded with protective hormones for Toby, I tentatively sat down with him on the sofa, holding him close. As usual, Buddy bounced up onto the sofa and snuggled in for a cuddle too, and he was so gorgeously gentle with my baby boy. He had a good sniff around and I'm sure he recognised Toby's scent from his blanket. Buddy was more curious than anything as he watched Toby sleeping.

"This is interesting, but does it do anything else?" he seemed to be asking me.

Susie, on the other hand, immediately lay on her side. Having previously had litters of puppies, she instinctively went into mummy mode, assuming the same position she'd taken when she'd had her own newborns to feed. It was so sweet. I truly believe that this was her way of saying she accepted Toby as a new member of our family.

It was wonderful to be home as a five-member family. Jon had two weeks' paternity leave, so it meant we had a bit of time to try to get the five of us into a new routine. It wasn't easy though, as Toby was still having difficulties feeding and was suffering with terrible reflux. Needless to say, I was terribly worried at the time, as I couldn't help thinking that it may turn out to be something serious. We later discovered it was a protein allergy. I'd been breast-feeding him, but the cow's milk I was consuming as part of my regular diet was affecting him.

Toby and I had a fair few sleepless nights during those first few weeks back home. Jon would occasionally take himself downstairs and sleep on the sofa bed with Buddy and Susie. I could hear them all snoring, and I must admit I was very jealous that they could all be so relaxed.

Toby was obviously now my number one priority. Thankfully, because Buddy and Susie had been there from the moment he came home, our baby boy always felt calm and safe with them. They all took to each other instantly, so when I saw a particularly cute baby grow for sale online, I just had to have it. It read: "My siblings have paws."

However confident I felt about the dogs being around Toby, I never left the baby alone with them. The dogs were never alarmed by his crying as they'd already been around enough friends' and relatives' babies to get used to them. Like everything else, they just took it all in their stride. But I was determined to make sure that neither of the dogs would get jealous of Toby. We didn't want them to ever feel shut out, so it quickly became a regular morning routine for the five of us to have cuddles on the bed. We still do it today, in fact, and you will often find the five of us all crammed on the sofa together too.

As always, Steven and the family rallied around and were a huge help. Those first few days back home from the maternity unit were a weird time for all of us, as we also had Dad's funeral and his house clearance to organise. Because Dad had been living in a bungalow, that was owned by the council, we only had a few days to clear out his flat so that someone else could move in. It didn't help matters that Dad had been quite a hoarder, and the place was full of computers, tools and electrical equipment. He always liked to have a tinker with machinery. Back in the day, before he was laid low with the cancer, he would have a go at mending anything.

I felt so useless, as I couldn't help with any lifting work after giving birth. Also, Toby was super-clingy to begin with and wanted me to hold him all of the time. He would cry every time I put him down, and he really didn't like being held by anyone else.

Dad's funeral was really hard for me. I'd been to plenty of funerals before, but emotionally I felt incredibly weak. I was overtired because of Toby, and I was grieving, not just for the person I'd got to know at the end of his life but also for the father figure I'd needed at the start of mine. I kept thinking that if it hadn't been for Buddy, we probably would never have had any more connection other than the same surname. As it was, I'd grown quite fond of the old devil, and our relationship had matured.

On the day of the funeral, my emotions were all over the shop. I was flooded with hormones, feeling the most intense love I'd ever felt before for my baby son. But I was really sad that I was having to say goodbye to the father I'd only recently started to know. It was a strange day for me. Funerals are never particularly pleasant. But I think I may have been able to handle it better if it had taken place a few months after giving birth rather than only after a few days. I was a wreck. I really felt like an orphan now that both Mum and Dad had gone.

The emotional
year continues

Having a newborn baby at home can be quite chaotic, to put it mildly. You think you've organised everything, covered every eventuality, but your plans quickly go out of the window once you actually get the baby home. Jon's paternity leave felt like it was over in a flash, and I soon found myself falling into a new routine. My life became Baby Central. It was exhausting and exhilarating at the same time: a wonderful, crazy blur of baby clothes and toys – and, in our case, dog toys.

Our little two-adult-two-dog family was loving having a new arrival, but I didn't want Buddy and Susie to miss out on their fun times now that Toby was around. Pets can get overlooked when a new baby comes along, so I was determined to make sure that wasn't going to happen with us. We decided right from the start that we would continue doing things that both humans and our dogs loved.

When Toby was just a few months old, Jon and I went along with our dog-show gang to Buckham Fair, a wonderful vintage dog and pony show in Dorset that's held in August. It's much bigger than the dog shows we normally go to and raises funds for a number of causes, including children's hospices and the air ambulance. We'd been talking about going for a few years. So a small thing like a tiny baby wasn't going to put us off making the journey.

"Wonder organisers" Neta and Jo had sorted out everything, so it was just a matter of the five of us getting in the car with all of Toby's paraphernalia. On the way there, we stopped off at Weston-super-Mare to take Buddy and Susie for a run on the beach and a splash in the sea with their friends. Buddy won't swim in the sea, but he loves chasing waves and charging around on the sand. It was a great way to break up the journey and get ready for what we knew would be an amazing time the following day.

Buckham Fair is a huge event with a funfair, great food stalls and fabulous horse and dog show activities. There are loads of daft, fun competitions to enter, including Temptation Alley, which is a race of willpower, Have a

Go Obedience Rings and the one that Buddy won, Best Biscuit Catcher. He seems to have a natural talent when it comes to food-related events. The event was hosted by the *Doc Martin* actor Martin Clunes and his wife Phillipa. He was there that day, along with his Jack Russell, Jim. Buddy was very excited to meet him – Jim, that is, not Martin.

We had a great time visiting all of the stalls and competitions, but the highlight of the day for all of us was when Tracy and Paul's lurcher Scout was named Rescue Dog Champion of Champions, winning the top prize of £350 for East Midlands Dog Rescue. Fay and I were so inspired by Scout's success that we entered Buddy and Fay's rescue Spanish Galgo Mila into the qualifying round for the following year's event. Mila has an amazing story: she'd been at death's door when she was rescued, having been left for dead in a field in Spain after being bludgeoned with a garden tool. Her injuries were horrific and it was touch and go if she would survive. But, like Buddy, the brave little fighter hung on. Her name Mila is short for Milagro, which is Spanish for miracle. She was brought to the UK and later adopted by Fay and Darrin.

As for our new little star, our beautiful Toby, he slept for most of the day and was as good as gold. Toby's first year really was a period of contrasts. In the winter, my wonderful Aunty Pat was diagnosed with throat cancer.

The news came as a terrible shock to all of us. She meant so much to everyone who knew her. She was the kindest person I'd ever known and had been like a mum to me, Michelle and Steven.

Aunty Pat was always thinking of others. She was the kind of person who would go out shopping, choose all sorts of things for other people and end up not buying anything for herself. She was completely selfless, one of a kind. She'd always been there for me. I have so many happy memories of her throughout my life: the time she made me a special dress when I was a little girl and I'd been told I couldn't be a bridesmaid; the time she made a garland for Buddy at our wedding; and, of course, the times she looked after Buddy for me. She was there to support and comfort me when I miscarried and later became pregnant with Toby. And those were just the big milestones; I have a lifetime of other memories of her too. It felt very raw to imagine life without her.

Aunty Pat's cancer was too advanced for treatments such as chemotherapy and radiotherapy to be of any benefit to her. So palliative care was her only option. Having been diagnosed in December 2017, tragically at Christmas, her health began to rapidly decline and she was transferred to a hospice to be cared for in her last days. Towards the end, I was getting up in the middle of the night to feed Toby and then leaving expressed milk for Jon to feed to him while I was with Aunty Pat at the hospice. It wasn't ideal, but I couldn't bear not being there for her. I could never repay her for all the love and tenderness she'd shown me throughout my life. But I wanted to be there for her as much as I could during her final days. I thought about taking Buddy in to see her too, but I decided that having an excitable hound bounding around a hospice full of terminally ill people probably wasn't a great idea.

On the day she died, Sunday 8 April 2018, I received a call early in the morning telling me that she was close to dying. I'd been on my way to see her, but I didn't make it to the hospice in time. Thankfully, she wasn't alone though. Michelle and Steven were there with other friends and family who adored her.

Her funeral was an emotional day for all of us. I've never been at a funeral so well attended. The crematorium was packed to the rafters and people were crammed into the foyer, spilling out into the courtyard. I felt very honoured to be invited to give a reading of the poem *You Can Shed Tears that She is Gone* by David Harkins. It ends with the words, "You can cry and close your mind, be empty and turn your back. Or you can do what she would want: smile, open your eyes, love and go on."

I thought these sentiments suited Aunty Pat perfectly.

She would never have wanted anyone to be upset. Aunty Pat was a wonderful woman, and I will always miss her.

Time to celebrate

No matter how tough life gets, when you have a tiny baby to care for, you have to find a way to work through your grief, to get on with life and celebrate the good times. We'd had a fair few emotional curve balls to negotiate during the past months, so it was good to have a happy event to look forward to – namely, Toby's naming ceremony on 13 May 2018.

Jon and I aren't religious. We wanted to host a celebratory day for Toby, but we didn't want a formal christening. Instead of godparents, we invited some of our special friends – Neta and Jo, Fay and Darrin, and an old friend of mine called Annette, who I first met when I started working at the job centre – to be Toby's guide parents. Toby wrote each of them a letter, asking if they would be happy to take on the role – okay, I admit it, I may have helped him a little bit – and I was chuffed to bits when they all agreed.

It was such a lovely day. Jon's grandmother, Marie, officiated at the ceremony, which took place at a beautiful old school in the village. Steven, who is a bit of a weekend disco king, provided the music. We had around 50 friends there, and we all got stuck into an enormous afternoon tea with loads of cakes. Jon's a bit of a "Great British Baker" on the quiet, and he made an amazing surprise cake with a pile of Smarties hidden inside it. Neta and Jo, meanwhile, covered a table with sweets and toys for the children, and we had an inflatable Wendy house that also went down a storm.

Our lovely baby boy slept through most of the day, but cleverly managed to keep awake for the ceremony, as he was named Toby Elliott David: Toby for no other reason than we liked the name; Elliott after a family that meant a lot to Jon; and David after Jon's father.

We wanted to keep things informal, but we asked Toby's new guide parents to read a poem or say a few words. Jo wrote a lovely poem about the day she and Neta met us at our first dog show, which really meant a lot to us. Here are a few lines of what she said:

Guidance and love will abound in a furry and human wraparound,

Toby will know compassion and care and will have The Crew to guide him there,

The walks with The Crew will shine sun on your face,

The dog shows will teach you dignity and defeat with grace,

along with charity, honesty, a laugh and a ribbon,

Toby, your bright smile will have everyone smitten.

Unfortunately, Toby's canine siblings weren't invited along on this occasion – all that chocolate would have been far too tempting. As any dog owner will confirm, human chocolate and dogs don't go together. Yet although Buddy wasn't with us, I was still mindful that we'd met our fantastic lifelong friends such as Neta and Jo and the rest of the gang because of him. It's why we continue to support rescue dogs whenever we can.

In August 2018, Buddy and I returned to Buckham Fair with Fay and Darrin, who brought their Saluki lurcher Jet (aka Jetty Spaghetti) and their Spanish Galgo Mila. Tracy was there too, with her 2017 rescue hero Scout. Buddy and Mila had qualified for the final of Rescue Dog of the Year. Could one of them possibly inherit Scout's crown?

There were around 70 canine finalists in the Rescue Dog of the Year category. There were heats scheduled throughout the day. These involved dogs and their owners going into the parade ring to meet with the judges. Buddy's heat went well, although I can't help feeling that I didn't sing my Buddy Dog's praises enough. I always enjoy telling people the story of how I first found Buddy, but I wish I'd also told the judges about the physical and mental impact he has had on me throughout my life. Rescue dogs sometimes have massive hurdles to overcome at the start of their lives, but Buddy also helped me to turn my life around.

Once our heat was over, Buddy and I were able to enjoy the other stalls and events at the fair. Very often, I don't choose the competitions we enter – Buddy does. "I like the look of that one!" he'll say, before, like a thing possessed, he'll drag me over to the action.

Today, he made it plain that he wanted to join in a hay bale jumping competition. The rules were simple: the dogs have to cross a run of hay bales and the fastest wins. My little Buddy went off like a rat up a drainpipe, bless him, but he wasn't in the same league as his long-legged canine competitors. He didn't get a placing, but he had the time of his life, which was the main thing. He was grinning like Batman's Joker after that.

Then it was time for the grand final of the Rescue Dog of the Year category. Martin Clunes kicked off the celebration by saying a few words and presenting each finalist with a lovely rosette. I thought that was a really nice touch, as rosettes are usually only given out to the winners and a number of runners-up.

The winners, as tradition demands, were announced in reverse order. Mila came in sixth place, winning a £50 voucher that Fay donated to Wellingborough Dog Welfare; Buddy Dog came fourth, winning a £100 voucher that we gave to the Senior Staffy Club. We were all thrilled to bits. Buckham Fair is such a special event and does so much to help spread the word about wonderful rescue dogs.

Buddy the Facebook star!

The crazy world of social media never ceases to amaze me. By the time Buddy made his first appearance at Crufts in 2016, he already had more than 20,000 Facebook followers. 20,000! It's bonkers, isn't it?

Buddy works hard to post regular updates about his life – okay, busted, I do it. But Buddy is generally in the room watching me at the time – and it's always a thrill to see all the "likes" and lovely comments that his photos get. From time to time, Jon and I also post video clips of Buddy that we think people will enjoy. To our utter amazement, one in particular has proved to be very popular indeed.

One day in October 2015, after Buddy's terrible year with cancer, Jon was on the floor at home rubbing Buddy's tummy. Now, our Buddy loves nothing more than a tummy rub. So each time Jon stopped rubbing him, Buddy reached out his paw and gently pulled Jon's hand back onto his tummy. Then he did it again. And again. Buddy just wouldn't let Jon stop giving him fuss.

It was hilarious. I grabbed my phone and started filming them. I tried to keep my hand steady, but it wasn't easy as I was laughing so much at our cheeky dog. I posted the clip on Buddy's Facebook page, and it immediately started getting lots of "likes" and laughing emojis. There were hundreds of them, then thousands. It was extraordinary. It had been lovely to capture Buddy's personality and share something that always made us laugh, but we couldn't believe how many other people were enjoying it too.

A couple of weeks later, I received an email from a Canadian video-sharing website, called Rumble, saying that they were interested in hosting Buddy's tummy-scratching film clip on their site. They weren't offering megabucks or anything, just a few pence here and there, but Jon and I thought, why not? Let's share the love. We always thought Buddy's tummy-rubbing routine was funny, but never in our wildest dreams did we ever imagine it would become an internet sensation. At the time of writing this book, more than nine million people have viewed the clip on

Facebook and over 65,000 people have liked it.

Other favourite videos on his Facebook page include "I'm a professional ball peeler", in which Buddy shows off his talent for removing the furry green cover from a tennis ball, with Susie Sausage looking on. She's concentrating so hard that it doesn't seem to bother her that Jon has balanced a stuffed chicken on her head. Another classic is "Buddy Dog's mad minute", where he keeps asking for tummy rubs, in between darting in and out of the room and giving a lightening-speed response to the question, "Are you hungry?"

Jon is often the co-star of Buddy's movies. You can tell he's trying to keep a straight face while our nutty dogs do what they do best – keeping us all entertained. Buddy, meanwhile, has bought himself a very comfy bed with his Rumble earnings, so he now looks more like the proper little celebrity he is.

As Buddy's Facebook following grew, he started receiving toys and gifts through the post, and we soon got to know our local postie, Faye. Buddy and Susie adore her: they both go mad with wagging tails and excited barking as soon as they see her red van coming towards the house. Luckily, Postie Faye adores them so much that she often brings them dog treats – one kind for Buddy and a special low-fat type for Susie – and will stop by to say hello even if she's out doing deliveries elsewhere in the neighbourhood.

It's lovely when people make the effort to get to know Buddy, as so many people are unsure about Staffies. When my friends and I go out fundraising with our dogs for East Midlands Dog Rescue, we love it when people come over to get to know our rescue hounds. The first year we did it was back in 2012, when we met for the first time at various dog shows that summer. Since then, we've thrown ourselves into it even more, with fancy dress costumes for the dogs, a tombola to win cuddly toys and toiletries, and carols at Christmas. The dogs will happily howl along too. Fundraising for East Midlands Dog Rescue has become such a regular event for us now, that Neta and Jo, Tracy and Paul, Fay and Darrin, Betty, Eluned, me and Jon call ourselves the EMDR Crew.

We now host our own annual charity dog show with all of our favourite events, including Dog Most Like Its Owner and Waggiest Tale, Best Rescue and Golden Oldie. Over the years, we've raised thousands of pounds. And because we have an independent judge, we can sign up our own hounds to take part too. We make money for the charity, and everyone gets to do what they love best. It's a win-win situation.

Susie is usually a bit take-it-or-leave-it when it comes to dog shows. She never "does a Buddy" and heads for a specific event; she would rather be off in Susie's World than joining in with something specific. However, at our EMDR show, we were thrilled when she won the Fastest Recall Event. We had independent judges, remember, so it was all fair and above board.

Because Buddy has made a bit of a name for himself, he also manages to wangle himself some nice freebies at dog shows. It can be a bit embarrassing at the time, but Buddy Dog has no shame. On one occasion, we were at a show at Stoneleigh Park in Warwickshire. Buddy headed straight to a posh clothing stand, which was selling special fleece dog coats and jumpers. It was in the middle of summer, so cold-weather gear may have been a hard sell – until Buddy offered to model it for them. His confidence seemed to have the desired effect. The woman on the stand gave him a cool T-shirt to wear. All she asked in return was that I directed anyone who asked about it over to their stand. I'm sure they had a lot of sales that day, as Buddy received lots of compliments.

Buddy's favourite dog shows are the ones where other animals are invited. That day at Stoneleigh was a particular highlight for him as it meant he could hang out with donkeys and loads of farm animals. Because of his early life at the stables, he loves to play with pigs and sheep, but he can get a bit over-excited and shouty. At another show we'd been to, he couldn't understand why he wasn't allowed in the pen with the sheep and goats.

"Why am I being kept separate?" he kept trying to ask us. "What's going on?"

As for Britain's second most popular pet, the cat, you may not be surprised to know that Buddy can be a scaredy cat himself when it comes to our feline friends. He gives our neighbours' big moggy a wide berth whenever he sees her. He knows his place after receiving a swipe from Lilly, one of the tabbies at the stables.

He may pretend he's fearless and run after cats if his other canine chums give chase, but he's never likely to catch one. And even if he did, he would soon show he's just a pussycat at heart. He actually purrs like a cat when he's stroked under his chin. How many Staffies can you say that about? He really is completely barking mad.

Our happy place

When we first met our dearest friends – Neta and Jo, Tracy and Paul, Fay and Darrin, and Betty and Eluned – little did we know that these eight people and their numerous hounds would play such an important role in our lives. We've gone through all manner of life's milestones together, from celebrations at dog shows, to the trauma of Buddy's cancer, human illnesses and bereavements. And that's just our own little family. Each of our friends has had their own challenges to face too. Having the support of a group of like-minded friends has been really special.

Sadly, some of our dogs are no longer with us, though quite a few new four-legged friends have joined us over the years. Floyd, Hero, Izzy, Mac, Indy, Ted and Cindy have all died since we got together, and while they can never be replaced, fuzzy Izzy, Sparky, Larry, Katie, Jet, Mila, Shadow and Bliss have all joined our wonderful group. Buddy and his gang happily accept any new fuzzy friends who come along with open paws, and they always have the time of their lives together. We're one big happy family.

The highlight of the year for all of us is when we go to Norfolk for a week's holiday in October. Neta and Jo have been going to Sea Palling, a lovely village on the East Norfolk coast, for several years and we've been hooked on the place since they introduced us to it. It's a tiny little seaside village, not showy at all, and it's perfect for dogs with its long stretch of sandy beach for them to sprint on to their hearts' content. It's also only a stone's throw from where we stay – we can see the ramp to the beach from the front door. As soon as Buddy and Susie get a sniff of the sea, their little noses start twitching and their stumps/tails start wagging: they know we've arrived at our happy place.

We rent a group of little cottages next to each other, with Neta and Jo, Jon, Toby and me in one of them, Fay, Darrin, Betty and Eluned next door, and Tracy and Paul in the third cottage along. On the canine front, there's Buddy and Susie, of course, plus Neta and Jo's lurchers Izzy and Gracie, at our cottage. Next door, there's Fay and Darrin's Saluki lurchers Bliss and Jet, their greyhound Shadow and their Spanish Galgo Mila, and Betty and Eluned's greyhounds Katie and Larry. Finally, at the third cottage, there's Tracy and Paul's lurcher Scout and their whippets Sparky and Misty. That's 74 legs in three little cottages. We bring the party!

Generally speaking, the dogs stay with their respective owners, but Buddy will often cuddle up with Neta and Jo in their room. He's always first to wake them up in the morning, whether they want to get up then or not. Bliss, meanwhile, is so relaxed and laid-back that she will sleep virtually anywhere. And we'll often find Katie, the most chilled-out greyhound I've ever known, upside down on a chair with her legs in the air. She's always so happy.

All the dogs feel so at home at Sea Palling, and they love nothing more than a long walk on the beach. Seeing them bombing around on the sand is always such a joy to all of us. With most of them being long-legged lurchers, whippets and greyhounds, poor Buddy doesn't have a chance in the speed stakes. But in true Buddy Dog style, he'll give it a good go, even sometimes helping other dogs if they're struggling. Buddy has so much stamina for such a chunky little dog. I don't think he realises that he's built differently to all of the others. He always looks puzzled about why he can't keep up with the champion runners and why he's always bringing up the rear.

Tracy and Paul's blind lurcher Scout has developed a special bond with Buddy. Sighthounds are dog breeds, such as lurchers and greyhounds, that naturally hunt by sight and speed. Scout loves to run with the other sighthounds, but he can't quite match their breakneck speed. He has a really high gait and runs rather like a Hackney horse, with quite elegant high steps. It's also not easy for Scout, as he can't see where he's going. But, because Buddy is such a noisy runner, as many Staffordshire Bull Terriers are, Scout can hone in on our Staffy's excited raspy breathing and run with some of the pack at least.

Lovely as it is to see Scout run with so much joy in his heart, he's also developed an over-exuberant habit of grabbing Buddy's stumpy tail when he catches up with him. Luckily, Buddy takes it all in his stride and never snaps about it. As Tracy once remarked, "To see these two survivors who have overcome the most horrendous start in life running side by side is a sight to behold and would melt the hardest of hearts."

Buddy is also great at teaching new dogs new tricks on the beach. Fay and Darrin have been adopting sighthounds for around 20 years, and it always takes them a while to train a new one to run off the lead. Sighthounds can cover great distances in a short space of time, and are nigh on impossible to catch if they run away. So it's crucial that you can completely trust them to come back to you before you let them off the lead.

Buddy has helped to teach Shadow and, more recently, Jet to run with confidence off the lead. He stays by their side to ensure they don't run too far away, and he rounds them up and brings them back if they start to veer off in another direction.

"Buddy is so calm and confident, helping them feel safe and to enjoy their first time off lead on a beach," says Fay. "Buddy knew just what he had to do, and now they are firm friends."

Buddy loves everyone, but he has a special place in his canine heart for Neta and Jo's dog Gracie, and they're never far apart. He also has a unique friendship with Tracy and Paul's whippet, Sparky. Bull breeds used to be Sparky's nemesis, but Buddy is the exception to the rule. Sparky will zoom around Buddy and hurl himself at him, and then does this strange action of offering his neck to him. Buddy, meanwhile, proceeds to repeatedly poke Sparky's neck with his nose and then does the canine equivalent of an eye roll.

Buddy really is totally unflappable. When Eluned introduced her new greyhound, Larry, to the gang, he started growling and barking at Buddy Dog. I expect it may have been because Buddy plonked himself on Eluned's knee and

Larry was getting a bit jealous. Luckily, though, no grudges developed and they're both happy campers together now.

As there are so many of us in the group, we don't do everything together during our Norfolk holiday. One day, a group of us may go somewhere like Sheringham or Cromer, and another day we'll go to Yarmouth or Holkham. Because we go every year, we've come to know the best dog-friendly beaches and the tide times, and have got to know some great walks – and lovely places for afternoon tea. Holkham Hall is a firm favourite, and the grounds there are fantastic for long dog walks. Buddy adores it.

Neta and Jo will happily look after Buddy and Susie if Jon and I want a day out with Toby. Sometimes they'll take Toby out for the day, and we'll stay back with all the dogs if they or any of the others want to visit places that don't allow our four-legged friends. No matter what we do during the day, though, we'll regroup in the evening at one of the cottages. Jo is an amazing cook so she's head of the kitchen, although several people will pitch in so that she gets a break from culinary duties.

All the dogs crash out together in the living room of whichever house we're in. All, that is, except for Buddy, who likes to have a seat at the dinner table wherever we are. I honestly think he nods along to our conversation and watches people speaking. I think he suffers from FOMO (fear of missing out!). One time I knew he was really sleepy, but he insisted on sitting at the table with us. He started nodding off, bumped his nose on the table and woke himself up. Anyone else would think it was probably time to say goodnight and take themselves off to bed, but not our Buddy. He just looks around as if to say, "Sorry, nodded off there for a moment. What have I missed?"

Susie, meanwhile, will be crashed out with the other dogs after a crazy run on the beach. I call her my Pocket Rocket, because she's a super-fast runner and does the typical gun-dog thing of running low, really close to the ground. She joins in with everything and is always so eager to please. It's almost as if she's worried that if she doesn't always try so hard, she'll no longer be wanted. This couldn't be further from the truth, of course. I hope Susie will realise that she'll always be safe and happy with us for the rest of her life.

After dinner, the cards and board games come out. There's Dog-Opoly, which, as it sounds, is the canine version of Monopoly where property is arranged by dog breed size – instead of going to jail, you get locked in a kennel. We also love Bugs in the Kitchen, which yes, is technically a children's game, but then we are all big kids at heart. The funniest game of all is Pie Face – especially when Buddy joins in. He'll do anything to get his snout crammed through the plastic mask in the hope of getting a pie thrown in his face.

Tracy says that there is something very human-like about Buddy. "His mannerisms and facial expressions can brighten up your day in an instant."

We generally don't have late nights because we like to make the most of the day – and Buddy always makes sure that no one gets a lie-in anyway. Whatever the weather, we'll put on our waterproofs – and waterproof dog coats for all the hounds – and off we'll go.

One day, Jon and I took Buddy to Blakeney Point to see the seal pups at their breeding point. We weren't sure whether dogs would even be allowed on the boat, but the boat crew were fine about him. They were obviously Staffy fans. When we arrived, there were so many seals that at first we thought they must be rocks on the beach, but then we saw them moving. There were hundreds and hundreds of them. They seemed as intrigued by us as we were about them. Straightaway, some of them came into the water and swam up to the boat to say hello. Buddy was in his element, with his nostrils flaring and his ears pricked up. It was as if he was saying, "Now this is new. What kind of dogs are these?"

I'd been anxious over how he was going to react to

seeing such a different kind of new animal, but as always, he took it all in his stride. Unlike some other Staffies that can be a bit skittish around other creatures, with Buddy, the more there are, the better. Because he was brought up at the stables, he's used to chickens roaming around freely. Whenever we visit a farm, he always runs up to say hello to any pigs, sheep and horses he can find.

As Toby grows up and new dogs join the gang, each Norfolk holiday will be slightly different. But for some reason, there's one thing that always manages to happen... There's a standing joke now that whether it's the first day, or the last day, Buddy will manage to trip Jo up. She's always taking photos – when she's not cooking, that is – and Buddy will always seem to get in the way. It's almost as if he sees her camera and thinks, "Right, I'll get her." She'll either step back and go flying backwards, or not see him smiling up at her and end up face down in the sand. Either way, it's always a good giggle for both of them.

All of us humans and canines see each other loads of times during the year, but the Norfolk holiday is the time when we can all relax and have a really good catch-up. It's great to be able to have a proper talk about everything, rather than only seeing each other when we're bombing around the country to dog shows or organising fundraising for local dog charities.

Sea Palling may not be the flashiest resort in the UK, and an October holiday may not be everyone's perfect time for a beach holiday, but going out of season means we generally have the whole beach to ourselves. It's our little piece of heaven. And when the holiday is over, and we have to get back home to normality, what's the best thing to do? Yup, we book the same three cottages for the following year. Well, it would be churlish not to.

Gotcha Days

I don't really remember having any happy birthdays when I was very young, at least not until I went to live with Aunty Angie and Uncle Rick. Now that I'm a mother myself, I want Toby to have all the things I missed out on, including lovely, fun family birthdays that I hope he can look back on fondly when he's older.

I have to confess that I occasionally go a bit over the top when it comes to the big day, though I doubt I'm the only mum who does that. Toby receives piles of cards and presents from relatives and friends. And then I'll always push the boat out at home with a birthday banner, cake for the humans and treats for the dogs, and silly hats for whoever would like to wear one.

It's the same, of course, for Buddy Dog and Susie Sausage. Very soon after I first found Buddy, I decided that, like every special creature on the planet, he should have a birthday. I appreciate that I don't know the actual date Buddy was born, but the vet estimated he was between six and nine months old on the day I found him. So I decided that 29 September should be his "official" birthday.

At one stage, the rest of the EMDR Crew and I used to buy presents for each other's dogs' birthdays, but it was all getting a bit out of hand, so we stopped. Nevertheless, Neta and Jo still turn up with a bag of toys and treats for Buddy and Susie. And as for Toby – well, as his guide parents, they love to make him feel even more special.

Birthdays aren't the only excuse we find to celebrate. Because of the joy that our rescue dogs have brought us, we also have Gotcha Day parties to celebrate the day they came into our homes. Buddy's Gotcha Day is 27 April. That's almost six months before his birthday, so it's nice that we have a reason to celebrate him on a couple of days each year.

Buddy's Gotcha Day means an awful lot to me, because my life changed forever – for the better – on the day I found him. As it's his day, we always try to do all the things he likes best. That means getting together with Neta and Jo and his other favourite people, a big walk with a game of frisbee, and lots of fuss, treats and presents – and, if it's chilly, a snooze by the wood-burning stove.

When we adopted Susie in June 2016, we had a "Welcome Susie" barbecue so she could get to know all of our best dog-mad friends and their respective canines. We decided on East Carlton Country Park, on the edge of the beautiful Welland Valley. We played games such as sausage bobbing, which is basically floating hot dogs in a trough of water and letting each dog have a go to find a piece. Susie wasn't too sure to start off with and growled a bit, but she soon got the hang of it.

We celebrate Gotcha Days for all of the dogs including Fay and Darrin's Saluki lurcher, Jet, aka Jetty Spaghetti. Before Fay and Darrin adopted him, the poor dog had been passed from pillar to post by several other owners. As a young stray, Jet had been taken to a dog pound, where he was given seven days to be claimed until he was euthanised. He was spotted and taken to East Midlands Dog Rescue for rehoming, but it didn't work out there. The poor boy went from one set of owners to another, before ending back in the Midlands.

Jet's now living the healthy, happy life he deserved. Fay and Darrin are his eighth stop and he's not even four years old yet – it's little wonder that he was so muddle-headed when they adopted him. In the same way that my life really changed when I found Buddy, Jet has made life complete for Fay and Darrin.

"Jet's Gotcha Day is 20 April," says Fay. "And because of the joy he's brought to our lives, we will always celebrate it."

While we make quite a thing of our pets' celebratory days, we're a bit more down to earth when it comes to the grown-ups. We're more likely to celebrate with a fish-and-chips supper or a walk and a picnic. And cake, of course. Always cake.

One birthday, Eluned bought me a consultation with a dog psychic for a bit of fun. The way that it works is that you send the psychic some photographs of your dog. Then they give a psychic reading based on what they see. Thank heavens they don't have to hypnotise the dog. Imagine trying to say to Buddy, "You are getting very sleepy."

Armed with the pictures, the psychic called me. We must have chatted for about an hour. I took it all with a pinch of salt, but one thing really resonated with me.

"Buddy wants you to stop changing his food," she said.

This was around the time when I was trying Buddy and Susie on different food combinations to find out what they liked and which was nutritionally best for them. It may have been guesswork, but the dog psychic got that bit right.

She then told me that Buddy calls me Snugger. *That's interesting,* I thought. *His favourite toy is his Wubba.* Again, I think I *may* have been reading rather too much into it. We talked about all sorts of other things as well – as you may have gathered, Buddy Boy is my favourite topic of conversation.

Before ending the session, I had one last question to ask her.

"Does Buddy know that I love him?"

"Yes, definitely," she said. "He says you tell him ALL THE TIME!"

2019... What a year!

In January 2019, for the second year running, ITV aired *Britain's Top 100 Dogs Live*, a countdown of the nation's most popular dog breeds. Settling down to watch the two-and-a-half-hour programme, I was sure that Springer Spaniels like my gorgeous Susie would rank high on the list, but I felt less confident about Staffordshire Bull Terriers. The breed has such a rotten reputation with Joe Public that I thought other, more cutesy breeds would poll much higher.

I hadn't watched the programme in 2018, but I wasn't surprised to learn that Labradors had come out on top in that list. I guess all of those Andrex puppies must have stolen the nation's hearts. Mixed breeds had come in second place that year, Jack Russells were third and Staffies, to my amazement, were fourth.

This year, I was determined not to miss it. I had my phone by my side. I knew all of my friends would be watching too so I expected us to all be texting each other while it was on. With more than 200 Kennel Club-recognised breeds and other dogs up for the title, I was interested to see where lurchers, whippets, greyhounds and cross-breeds ranked. Not that it mattered; it wasn't as if our dogs' popularity scores were going to make us love them any more or any less than we already did. Any programme about how wonderful dogs are is good in my book, and it would be a good watch wherever they came in the countdown.

The list of the 100 most popular breeds was compiled using a survey of 10,000 people, with the order of the top 10 being voted on by viewers on the night of the programme. As the programme, presented by Sara Cox and Ben Fogle, counted down from 100th place, I was a little surprised to see Rough Collies come in at 65 and Yorkshire terriers at 54. When they announced that Schnauzers were at 44 and French Bulldog were at 42, I began to think there was some very odd voting going on. I'd assumed that these breeds would be much more popular with the general public.

Greyhounds ranked 40th – boo, not high enough! – followed by whippets at 39 and lurchers at 37. What was going on? Why don't people realise what amazing dogs our fuzzy friends are? As the time came to announce the order of the top 10, I was beginning to regret not voting. But I'd been a little preoccupied with our gorgeous wriggly Toby, who was wedged on the sofa with me, Jon, Buddy and Susie.

Each time a breed was announced, I kept saying "Staffies will be next", never thinking for a moment that they would come higher than beautiful Springer Spaniels. The 10th place went to mixed breeds, 9th to Golden Retrievers, 8th to German Shepherds and 7th to Border Collies. The 6th place went to Boxers, with Cocker Spaniels coming in 5th and Springer Spaniels were 4th. Susie looked very pleased at that result, but then again, she often looks as if she's smiling.

Last year's winner, the Labrador, came in 3rd place, which meant that the Staffordshire Bull Terrier or the Cockapoo would take the title.

"That's that, then," I said to Jon, "there's no way Staffies will ever beat Cockapoos."

After all, Cockapoos always seem to be picking up beauty contest trophies, and loads of celebrities have them because they're so adorable looking. Then – drum roll, please – it was announced that Britain's favourite breed of dog for 2019 was the Staffordshire Bull Terrier. I couldn't believe it!

The programme featured clips of celebrities talking about their four-legged friends, including *Coronation Street* actor Sue Cleaver and her rescue Staffy, George Paws. She adopted George in 2014 and had, like me with Buddy, always assumed he was a mixed breed. Just as I'd also done with Buddy, she submitted George for a DNA test, which revealed that he was 100 per cent Staffy.

Summing up, Sara Cox said, "With courage, intelligence and a love of children being just some of their best traits, it's no wonder that the Staffy is our top dog this year." She went on to say, "Despite being in this year's top 10, as a breed, the Staffy is faced with a very sad problem…"

The programme explained how there are more Staffies in rescue homes than any other type of dog breed. An RSPCA spokesperson said: "Unfortunately, Staffies have received a lot of bad press in recent years due to irresponsible people using them as status dogs and treating them really badly, so it can take us longer to re-home Staffies than other types of dogs in our care because of those misconceptions that people have around the breed. But once people come into our centres, they get to know that they are really sweet, loving dogs. Every dog deserves a second chance to find a good home."

I had mixed feelings about the result, I admit. Naturally, I was thrilled that Staffies had been recognised as such wonderful dogs – I've been saying the same thing for years, after all – and I hoped that it would mean more people would actively go to rescue centres to adopt a Staffy. I knew they definitely wouldn't regret it if they did. But I was also concerned that idiots who aren't proper breeders would start breeding Staffies purely as a means of making money. This, sadly, has happened in the past when breeds have won Best in Show at Crufts.

I hope it goes without saying that I think top-class Staffies, with their beautiful temperaments and breed-standard looks, should continue to be bred in moderation, as we don't want to lose them. But there are a lot of backyard breeders out there, and that's where the problems start with interbreeding and poor levels of health care. Too many unscrupulous breeders cross-breed Staffies with pit bulls and other aggressive dogs, and the resulting "Status dogs" continue to give the breed a bad name.

In March 2019, it was time for one of Buddy's favourite events of the year – and one of mine too –Discover Dogs at Crufts. We were thrilled to be going again, especially as we hadn't been invited to attend in 2018. I'd initially been concerned that this may have been because of something Buddy had done. But it turned out that it was because they thought I already had enough on my plate looking after Toby. As if that would ever have stopped us!

Needless to say, I was delighted when the East Anglian Staffordshire Bull Terrier Club said they would like to have Buddy along again. We proudly announced the news on his Facebook page, and the post received lots of comments and "likes". So we knew it was going to be a busy couple of days.

Buddy was totally at ease from the moment we arrived. As soon as we walked through the doors into the main hall at the NEC, he made a beeline for his favourite food stands. We made sure we were ready to answer questions on the Discover Dogs stand, and more people than ever came up to say hello and ask for selfies. It may, I think, have had something to do with the ITV poll. As usual though, Buddy took it all in his stride and happily allowed himself to be patted, cuddled, posed with, filmed and, of course, rewarded with treats.

A girl working on a very premium food stand fell head-over-heels in love with Buddy. He'd been wearing his very handsome striped bow tie and collar when he met her, so it was hardly surprising. Later, she wrote on his Facebook page, "I cried on the train home tonight because I missed Buddy."

What did surprise us though was the newspaper

coverage that Buddy received the following day. In one paper, there was a massive picture of Buddy with the headline 'ABUSE HELL BUDDY SHOWS AT CRUFTS'. The story was all about how I'd found him and how he was championing Staffies at Discover Dogs. Incredibly, the story about Buddy was bigger than the story about the year's Best in Show at Crufts.

It took me a few minutes to twig how I'd ended up in the papers. I then remembered that a journalist called Rachel Spencer had contacted me about Buddy's story for her blog, *The Paw Post*. She'd been writing a story about hero Staffies and, like everyone who meets Buddy, had fallen in love with him. Then, on the weekend of Crufts, the newspaper had picked up on her lovely story, and Buddy was suddenly headline news.

All of a sudden, I was getting phone calls from people I hadn't heard from for ages, and Buddy's Facebook page was on fire. It was lovely to read comments such as, "Well done for highlighting rescues and Staffies", and, "Well done, Buddy. Shows Staffies are the best. Great news on rescues."

There was even more excitement to come. A couple of weeks later, out of the blue, I received an email from a book publisher saying they were interested in Buddy's story. I couldn't believe it. The publisher wanted me to write about how I found Buddy and about all of the ups and downs in his life – and mine. How could I resist?

What's next for us?

It's been lovely re-living old times with Buddy, but I still shed a tear when I look at the picture I took of him on the day I found him. Who would have thought that 10 years would be so momentous? It's certainly been a journey for both of us.

Buddy turns 11 in September. Although he's still full of energy and fun, I know that the years are beginning to catch up with him. Suffice to say, I don't think he'll be climbing any more mountains. I've noticed lately that he's starting to slow down a bit, and I recently bought him a pet buggy. It means that in the future, if we're out on a walk and it starts to get too much for him, he can have a little rest without missing out on anything. As long as he's got his wheels, he can be as mobile as the rest of us and still enjoy being with his friends.

No matter how many years Buddy has left – and I dearly hope that there are *many, many* more – I'm determined to make sure that these are as healthy and happy as possible. I'll continue to take Buddy to dog shows for as long as I think he's enjoying them, but I'll nip them in the bud if he starts to look fed up. I can't imagine he ever will though, as he loves seeing all of his friends and being around people.

Looking ahead, we're hoping to extend our human family, and I'm always hinting to Jon that I would like more dogs in our household. Every time I help re-home a breeding bitch or an unwanted puppy, I think, *Hmm, maybe... I'm sure he or she would instantly be welcomed by the EMDR Crew.*

Buddy will continue his Facebook page and, hopefully, will be invited to Discover Dogs at Crufts again. I'm so proud that he's been able to be an ambassador for Staffies and spread the word about how fantastic the breed is.

I hope you've enjoyed our story together. Most importantly, if you weren't sure about Staffies before, I hope I may have helped to change your mind about them. At the end of this book, there's information about adopting a rescue dog. Who knows – maybe your own Staffy adventure will begin soon?

Buddy facts

What Buddy has taught me

Over the years, I've tried to teach Buddy a few tricks. When he was much younger, I taught him all the basics – sit, stay, leave and so on – and, as you will know by now, he quickly became a great frisbee catcher. He's also a dab hand at high-fiving people and rolling over, and during the last couple of years he's learned how to weave in and out of my legs. Clever Buddy Dog.

I sort of wish I'd taught him more tricks over the years. I always love watching dogs do dance routines on shows such as *Britain's Got Talent*, but Buddy has become more stubborn about learning new moves as he's got older. I think it may be a bit too late for him to get a slot on *Strictly Come Dancing* too, though he would look great in all of the outfits. Then again, he continues to surprise me every day.

What Buddy has taught me, and what he continues to teach me, is that you can never judge a book by its cover. Who would have thought that a dog at death's door who had clearly been mistreated could have a heart of gold and the best nature in the world?

Buddy has shown me that kindness can come naturally, and that it costs nothing to give people a smile – a smile that can make the whole day better. Yes, okay, I know Buddy is a dog, but he's certainly not just a dog to me. He's been a real friend, a warm, sturdy body to cry on when I've needed one, and a daft clown to cheer me up when I'm feeling down.

Sometimes, after a hard day, all I need to hear is the clip-clip-clip of his little legs running down the hallway as I step through the front door, and I'll instantly de-stress. He'll drop a ball at my feet and look at me as if to say, "Come on, let's play," and five minutes later I'll be running around the garden with him without a care in the world. It's the same with my Susie Sausage.

I've come to realise that, my close friends and family aside, I think I love animals more than I do people. Animals love you unconditionally and aren't concerned about getting anything back – aside from a dog treat or two.

I was there for Buddy at the start of his new life, and

he's always been there for me ever since. I've been through the heartache of miscarriage and losing several people close to me, not to mention that traumatic episode of nearly losing Buddy to cancer. But my plucky little dog has taught me resilience and strength, supporting me with a little raised ear and a waggy stump.

"Don't worry Mum," I can almost hear him say, "it's all going to be okay."

For many years, my life was only about me and doing what I wanted to do to keep myself happy. I suppose that all started because I felt so alone when I was growing up. Through Buddy, I've learned that I have to take responsibility for others, as well as for myself. Taking care of horses helped me understand the care and dedication needed to help an animal thrive. Looking after Buddy – and then Susie and now Toby – has cemented this ability to put others first. I had to grow up quite quickly. In the beginning, it was just me. Now it's all about my human and animal family.

I hope Buddy has managed to change a few other people's minds about Staffics too. They're not threatening fighting dogs that should be avoided, but fun, loving, dedicated souls that are fantastic with children and make wonderful companions. And in Buddy's case, especially older ladies with a love of *Downton Abbey*.

Through having Buddy in our lives, Jon and I have made a wonderful set of friends who mean the world to us. So much so, that our annual holiday to Norfolk is our favourite part of the year, when all of our crazy canines and fuzzy friends get together to run on the sand and prove the best things in life are free. Buddy may not be able to run as fast as his friends, or win Crufts Best in Show, but I couldn't love him more.

Thank you, Buddy x

Buddy facts

Adopting a rescue dog

If Buddy's story has made you think about getting your own rescue dog, that's great news. Because so many people only want pedigree puppies or designer crossbreeds, "bitsas" and mongrel dogs can struggle to find owners. And when it comes to imperfect damaged goods such as Buddy Dog, and some of the neglected cases you'll have read about in this book, it's even harder for them to find loving homes.

Even if you don't know of one yet, it won't be hard to find a rescue centre near you. The Dog's Trust (www.dogstrust.org.uk) is the UK's largest dog welfare charity and has a network of 21 rehoming centres across the UK and Ireland. They care for around 17,000 dogs every year, so there are always plenty to choose from.

The RSPCA (www.rspca.org.uk) has 17 regional centres across England and Wales for adoption and rehoming, and Battersea (www.battersea.org.uk) has three rehoming centres: London, Windsor and Brands Hatch. These are just the big names out there. Depending on where you live, you'll find loads of other great local dog rescue shelters. Many councils re-home dogs collected as strays or abandoned locally, so it's worth doing a thorough search online and via your local vet for a shelter near you.

Things to consider first

Before you go out to look for any kind of new four-legged friend, whether it's a pedigree champ or a rescue mutt, there are various factors you need to consider. Being practical, what kind of dog will suit you and your family? How much space do you have at home? Have you owned a dog before?

Having any kind of dog can be a lot of hard work, so you need to be sure that you've thought everything through. You'll need to do your homework before you start thinking of cute names and what colour collar you're going to buy. It's not just a matter of who will take it out for walks. Do you have the time and commitment to make it feel happy at home? Can you afford it? As I found out many times with Buddy and Susie, vet bills can be very expensive. Do you go away a lot? Are any family members allergic to dogs or nervous with them? Does your lease allow you to keep animals on your property?

What type of dog will you get?

The main difference between adopting a rescue dog and taking on a pedigree puppy is that you may not know much about its history. Dog shelters ask for as much information as they can when they take in an animal for rehoming – about its parents, its temperament and any health issues that need to be considered – but you have to remember that rescue dogs can have all sorts of history and some information can be quite sketchy.

They may have lived happily in a family home, but for one reason or another they can no longer be kept as a pet. Or they may have been used as a breeding bitch, a working dog or a racing dog and have "outgrown their use". Whatever the circumstances, rescue dogs may need extra special tender loving care. They may have developed behavioural traits that need to be considered, such as separation anxiety. You'll need total commitment.

Many people don't like the idea of taking in an older dog, but these can often have better manners than a puppy. As well as being more likely to come housetrained, they may not need as much exercise as a younger dog and they can be calmer and more relaxing to have around. The Dog's Trust says, "When rehoming an older dog, what you see is what you get. His personality has already been shaped so there should be no surprises in the future."

What does the adoption process involve?

What may surprise you is that before you can take any dog home, you have to be vetted too. It's not just a matter of walking into an animal shelter, choosing a cute pooch and off you go. The process varies from one animal rescue organisation to another, but most will involve the following steps:

Register your details

This will mean answering a set of questions about your current living circumstances.

Visit the centre

The rehoming team will follow up your initial application with a face-to-face chat to understand your needs. Be aware though that your needs won't necessarily match the needs of the dog you want to take home.

You may have already shown interest in a dog you've seen online, but often the dog will choose you rather than the other way around. The Dogs Trust says that people often visit with an idea of the kind of dog they want and end up going home with something completely different. It's good to be flexible. Ask lots of questions and be as upfront as you can, so that the rehoming team can help to match up dogs with the most suitable owners.

Prepare for home visit

Many shelters will visit your home to check you can provide the right environment for the dog. Don't worry, they're not going to judge your lampshade choice. They'll probably ask you about what you're likely to be feeding the dog, how much exercise it will get, the length of periods a dog may be left alone and how secure your garden is, if you have one. This is to check that you're totally committed to having a new four-legged friend. It will be more like a friendly chat than a daunting interrogation. It's all about what's best for the animal.

Most adoption and rehoming centres are run as charities, so a donation will be expected if you end up taking a dog home. It's money very well spent, as in nearly all cases your dog will have had a full medical check-up and will be microchipped, vaccinated and neutered. The centre may also provide you with a starter pack of food and some free pet insurance.

Settling in your new family member

When you bring the new member of your family home for the first time, be prepared for some adjustment time. It may not be completely plain sailing from the outset. The new dog may walk in, pee on the carpet, eat your favourite shoes and zoom around like a loony, barking at everything they see.

You may already be thinking, "Uh-oh, what have we done?" But don't panic. Your dog comes with its own personality, habits and quirks that you may not have picked up on when you first met. Here are four ideas to help the transition:

Take it slow

Just as we humans need time to adjust to new surroundings, so do dogs. Let them explore the house and garden at their own pace. If your dog has come from a noisy kennels environment, it may be exhausted and need to sleep a lot to begin with. Don't over-stimulate your new four-legged friend. If they appear a bit standoffish, it's only because they're getting used to their own surroundings. Let them come to you for affection to begin with, rather than crowding them out. Not all dogs bond with a new owner immediately. Don't take it personally, and just give it time.

Give your dog space
Provide your dog with their own comfy bed, and he'll soon have his own smells there to comfort him. Some dogs just need a bit of time to chill out and relax if they've been in another environment for a while. Work at their pace and allow them to feel part of the home. Just as you may have a favourite room to retreat to, it's lovely for your dog to have their own zone too. Help your dog settle in with a treat hidden inside a Kong Ball, so the activity of finding it acts as a diversion. It also shows that you're the provider of nice things, which will help them to trust you more.

Be prepared for tummy troubles
Accidents are bound to happen when your new four-legged friend arrives. Nerves, discombobulation and a change in diet are all to blame. When it comes to your dog's diet, if you don't like the idea of the food they were eating before, try mixing some of the old food with the new so that it tastes familiar. Diarrhoea is very common during the first couple of days in a new environment, but consult your vet if it continues for more than a few days. To avoid any house training issues, take your dog out regularly.

Be patient
Just as we all need time to adapt to new surroundings and

routines, so will your dog. Don't expect everything to be perfect straight away. Take things slowly, consider what an upheaval the whole experience is for them, and before you know it, you'll have a great new best friend.

Children's safety

The RSPCA has six golden rules for keeping your child safe and your dog happy.

1. Never leave your child alone in the same room as a dog, even your own.
2. Teach your child never to approach a dog when it's eating a treat, playing with its toy, sleeping, unwell, tired, blind or deaf.
3. Teach your child to be kind and polite to dogs. Don't let your child climb on dogs, pull their ears or do anything you wouldn't allow them to do to another child.
4. Teach your child how to play nicely with your dog.
5. Supervise your child when they're with your dog. If the dog looks unhappy, let the dog go somewhere it feels safe and happy.
6. Never allow your child to approach a dog they don't know.

Finally, don't forget Lucy's Law.
If you have your heart set on a puppy, you can give it the best start in life by remembering Lucy's Law.

Only buy a puppy if:
- You can see your puppy interacting with its mum.
- Its breeder is recommended by the Kennel Club (preferably an Assured Breeder).
- It's from a rescue centre that's a registered charity.

Be suspicious of a puppy-farmed pup if:
- Its mum isn't there whenever you visit the puppy. She may be miles away on a cruel puppy farm.
- The price is very cheap (say, £100 to £350), or very expensive (£2,000 to £7,000).
- The puppy is being sold in a pet shop or garden centre and not at an approved breeder's home.

Hello everyone, I'm Buddy!

I hope you enjoyed reading the story of how my human mum Nicola found me, and nursed me back to health and gave me the great life I have now.

Back in 2009 when Nicola found me I really was in a terrible state as my previous owners had left me out in the cold to die. They'd put me in a tiny crate so I couldn't run away, and with no food or water, I really thought my days were numbered.

But just when I was on my last legs, Mum Nicola came along and turned my life around. She saw I was still breathing, just, and decided right there and then that she was going to look after me. It turns out that she's always been crazy about animals, so it really was my lucky day. She wrapped me in a towel and said, "I've got you now, Buddy. You'll be okay." Even though the vet wasn't sure I was going to make it, Mum was determined that I would pull through and gave me lots and lots of tender loving care.

If you look at the picture she took of me on the day she found me, you'll see that I haven't always been the handsome dog I am now. But with her patience and kindness, I eventually bounced back to health. I've climbed Snowdon, won trophies at dog shows and was even asked to represent Staffies at Crufts' Discover Dogs. I've made loads of friends along the way, and I even have my own social media site with more than 26,000 followers.

We've had some amazing times together, even though my tail had to be cut off, I nearly choked at a dog show and then I had cancer. Meanwhile, Mum Nicola has had all sorts of family dramas and tears throughout the years too. But whatever life has thrown at us, through good times and bad, we've always had each other. She rescued me, but I believe that we rescued each other.

I hope you enjoyed our story. Right, I'm off to play frisbee now.

Buddy Dog

Acknowledgements

When I began writing this book, some episodes, such as the day I found Buddy, came back to me in a flash. When it came to recalling my early life, I would like to thank my brother Steven and sister Michelle, who were able to jog my memory and help me fill in lots of the blanks. They've always been such a massive part of my life, along with Angie and Rick and Sally and Rob. I can't thank you enough for all that you've done for me. I would like to thank Aunty Pat too. She isn't with us anymore, but she will always be in the line-up of amazing people in my life.

To all of the EMDR Crew, thank you so much for all of the phone calls, texts and emails reminding me of all the funny stories and great times we've had with Buddy Dog.

You've all been incredibly supportive and positive about the project. A huge thank you too, to Jo Green for letting me use lots of her photographs, and to Nigel Ord Smith (*www.nigelordsmith.com*) and Andy Biggar (*www.andybiggar.com*) for allowing me to use their professional photographs.

Thanks to East Anglian Staffordshire Bull Terrier Club for considering Buddy for Discover Dogs, to all of Buddy's Facebook followers for their support, to everyone I have named in the book, and to Nicole Carmichael and Jonathan Bowman for their help with writing it. And a huge thank you to Ajda Vucicevic and the whole team at Mirror Books, for recognising how special Buddy is and making this book a reality.

Finally, and most importantly, thank you to Jon for your patience and kindness in life generally, especially while I've been writing this book. Toby and I (and baby number two!) love you very much.

Buddy Dog
AND
Susie Sausage